A History of Playing Cards

A History of

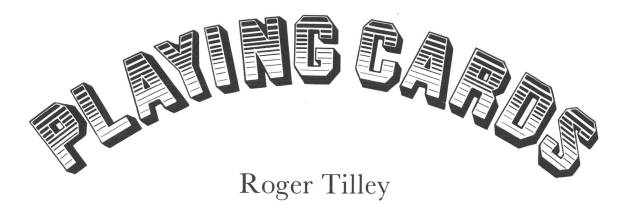

PLAYING CARDS

Roger Tilley

 Clarkson N. Potter, Inc./Publisher NEW YORK
Distributed by Crown Publishers, Inc.

This book is dedicated to *Evelyn Goshawk,* but for whose kindness in working on the script, coupled with enthusiasm and hard work, it might never have been published.

Copyright © 1973 the estate of Roger Tilley

Published in 1973 by Clarkson N. Potter, Inc., Publisher, New York.

Library of Congress Catalog Card Number: 73-75005
ISBN: 0–517–50381–6
Printed in Great Britain

Contents

Chinese playing cards derived
from old paper money. Suits of
coins, strings of coins and
myriads of strings of coins.
Bodleian Library, Oxford

6

1   Origins of playing cards

Legends step in where historians fear to tread. Just as a squint enabled an observer to pierce the chancel wall and watch the high altar, so legends, many of which may be regarded with respect, if not with unqualified belief, provide historians with a peep-hole through the wall of mist surrounding pre-history. As the origins of playing cards are hidden from us by the screen of at least six centuries, it is certainly important, and possibly profitable, to examine the relevant legends. There are two.

Part-time occupation and never more in a whole life-time's employment, was the 'eating canker' in the lives of the queens and concubines of an eastern harem. Unmitigated boredom, according to one legend, and irritability arising from unmitigated boredom, according to the second, resulted in the harem becoming the cradle of playing cards.

In the first legend 'the inner chambers' of the Chinese imperial palace are said to have seen the birth of cards. The 'veiled ones' secluded therein were numerous, since the Emperor had not so much a wife as a bedroom staff, for which the recognized establishment for some two thousand years was: Empress 1, Consorts 3, Spouses 9, Beauties or Concubines 27, and Attendant Nymphs or Assistant Concubines 81. The numbers 3 and 9 were held in particular regard by the astrologers. See also colour illustration page 33

The 'mistresses of the bed' kept regular night watches, the 81 Attendant Nymphs sharing the imperial couch for 9 nights in groups of 9, the 27 Beauties 3 nights in groups of 9, the 9 Spouses and 3 Consorts 1 night per group, and the Empress 1 night alone.

These arrangements lasted from, roughly, the early years of the Chou dynasty (112–255 BC) to the beginning of the Sung dynasty (AD 950–1279) when the old order broke down and had to be abandoned according to a contemporary post, because of the unbridled and ferocious competition of no less than 3000 ladies of the palace. After making every allowance for poetic licence, it is clear that by the time of the Sung dynasty the occupants of the 'inner chambers' had even less to do than ever before, and time must have been wearisome to the point of inducing mental breakdown. As a result, says the legend, in the year AD 1120, playing cards were conceived by an inmate of the Chinese imperial harem, as a pastime for relieving perpetual boredom.

The second legend attributes the invention of playing cards to the fretful wife of an unidentified but fidgety Indian Maharajah. For her, too, time had leaden feet, even if the royal sleeping staff was smaller

7

by far than at the imperial palace in China. In this case, boredom, already protracted and apparently unending, made the queen excessively irritable, with the result that her husband's trick of continually pulling at his beard frayed her nerves beyond endurance. Seeking a means of countering his distressing habit she, it is claimed, hit upon the idea of an indoor game which would not only occupy his mind but keep his hands engaged. Wherefore, according to the second myth, playing cards were invented.

These two legends are far from straining credulity. They may, indeed, hold more than a grain of truth; for the ladies of the harem not only had urgent need for some such invention but had the necessary time to give to the matter, and, what is even more important, included in their circle women of talent. The very air they breathed was, no doubt, full of the germs of fancy. Moreover, so far as the Chinese legend is concerned there are two further points which appear to be relevant. The first is that the Emperor Hui Tsung, who reigned from AD 1100–25, was a painter of the first rank and a noted calligrapher. Could he not have sympathized with his women-folk and lent his brush to the enterprise? The second point is that the period was one of the finest in the history of printing from woodblocks in China.

Games have seldom, if ever, been invented in the true sense of the word, but have been evolved over a period of time from vague and unidentified beginnings. If playing cards were in fact first enjoyed in the harem, it is probable that like many western games they were influenced by some ritual of divination, or some accustomed fertility rites of their age. 'Oats, peas, beans and barley grow', played by American children is almost certainly a survival of an ancient religious ceremony calculated to make the fields fertile. 'London Bridge is broken down', is thought by that great authority on songs, Lady Gomme, to recall the custom of immuring living beings in the foundations of a bridge in order to preserve it from the malice of the spanned river.

And so we may assume that if playing cards were in fact born in the harem it is more than likely that the inventive lady, or ladies, fashioned her, or their, pastime from some fertility rite, calculated to call down fruitful blessings on the imperial or royal couch, or from some ritual of divination employed to foretell the outcome of the night watch.

However that may be, the early history of playing cards is not solely a matter of legend and guesswork, nor is it confined to China and India. At least two authorities, Sir William Wilkinson and Dr Stewart Culin, were of the opinion that Chinese cards are descended from Korean, and that Korean, in their turn, are descended from the Korean divinatory arrow and the way in which it was used. They based their views on the examination of, and reasoning from, actual cards.

Sir William Wilkinson (1858–1930) made his career in the British China Consular Service, from which he retired in 1918. While so employed he became a noted collector and student of Chinese playing cards and also wrote several books under the pseudonym of Khanoo. *The Game of Khanoo* and the appropriate pack were published by Charles Goodall and Son, the playing card printers, in 1891; and two editions of *Bridge Maxims* were brought out in Hong Kong in 1918, with a third edition in England, also published by Charles Goodall & Son, in 1920. Sir William also wrote a paper for the January 1895 issue of the *American Anthropologist* entitled 'The Chinese Origin of European Playing Cards'; and in 1896 he published a book on some aspects of the Korean Government.

Dr Culin, who was born in 1858 and died in 1929, was Director of the Museum of Archaeology and Palaeontology at the University of Pennsylvania, his peculiar discipline being ethnology within which he made a particular study of Asiatic games. He was the author of *Korean Games, The Gambling Games of the Chinese* and *Chess and Playing Cards*. The last was a catalogue of, and report on, the museum's collections of those items which were shown at an international exposition at Atlanta, Georgia, in 1895. So far as the cards were concerned the exhibits were mostly from the Wilkinson collection, on permanent loan to the museum.

According to Dr Culin, the standard Korean pack consisted of eight suits of ten cards each, though the number of suits was reduced to six, or even four, according to the number of players. The eight suits were *Sa răm* (man), *Moul-ko-ki* (fish), *Ko-ma-koui* (crow), *Koueng* (pheasant), *No Ro* (antelope), *Pyel* (star), *Htoki* (rabbit) and *Măl* (horse). The tenth card in each suit was called *tjyang* (general). The two most popular games were *Yet-Pang-Mang-I* and *Tong-Tang*; others were *Ka-Keui* and *Net-tjyang-ke-ri*. The cards were made of oiled silk and were up to 8 inches long and $\frac{1}{4}$ to $\frac{1}{2}$ inch wide.

Chinese cards varied considerably, and while smaller than the Korean were still long and narrow, being up to nearly 5 inches long and $1\frac{1}{2}$ inches wide. Sir William divided Chinese games into seven classes, three based on money or money tokens, and one each on cash, dominoes, Chinese chess and 'miscellaneous' respectively.

The commonest packs were two of the first group, *Kwan p'ai*, (stick cards) and *Lüt chi* (waste paper), both of which were made in several forms. The former had three, and the latter four, suits of ten cards each, the values being 1 to 9 together with a court card. The suits were *ts'in* or cash (sometimes *ping* or cakes), *sok* or strings of cash, and *man* or myriads of strings of cash in the *Kwan p'ai* pack, to which *lakhs* or tens of myriads of strings of cash was added in the case of *Lüt chi* cards. The suits were identified by different symbols, and the backs were usually plain though they sometimes had a diamond pattern. In some cases a special mark was shown at each end of the card, making them, in effect, double-ended, a design detail which did not become general in the west until the second half of the nineteenth century.

The two experts give several reasons for believing that Korean

Ganjifa pack, Indian Mogul
style, hand-painted and gilded
on ivory.
Bodleian Library, Oxford

cards were derived from the divinatory arrows: firstly, their shape, since they appear to be modelled on the slips of bamboo used as arrows in the ritual of divination; second, a heart-shaped scroll on the backs, which was thought to be a representation of an arrow feather; and third, the belief that the numerals on the cards are survivals of the cock feathers of the original arrows. That Chinese cards are, in their turn, descended from Korean is deduced from their similar arrow-like shape; also the marks at the card-ends are thought to be adaptations of the Korean feather numerals. Moreover, the larger Chinese packs can also be reduced to six or four suits according to the number of players. Similarities in nomenclature occur: the Korean for cards is *htou-tjyen*, meaning fighting-tablets (literally bamboo slips used for writing), of which the Chinese equivalent is *tsau-ts'in*, while the money symbols on Chinese cards are called *ts'in*. The eighty numbered lots used for divining lucky numbers in a lottery, and which almost exactly duplicate the Korean pack, are called *ts'in*.

Dr Culin gives no date for the first appearance of Korean cards; but he does remark that the pictures on some of the higher Chinese cards appear to have been taken from a novel written by Shi Nai Ngan at some time in the Yuan dynasty (AD 1280–1368).

The argument that European cards are descended from the Chinese is based on the supposition that, through ignorance of their real meaning, the symbols identifying the suits became progressively corrupted in copying until, eventually, they crystallized into the suit-signs of the early European cards. Even with a lively imagination this is difficult to see; but the big hurdle that this theory has never surmounted is that during the whole course of more than half a millenium not one actual card which illustrates the point has yet come to light. At best, therefore, it remains a theory, and it is regarded with suspicion by modern scholarship.

Where Chinese cards are black and white, as straight and narrow as a moral principle, and are concerned only with sordid cash, Indian cards are round and brightly painted and devoted to a religious theme. In the absence of any theory of development from an earlier form, we are left with the legend of the restless Maharajah and the sensitive Maharenee. And if there be any truth in the story, the source of the Maharenee's inspiration is much as would be suspected: for religion may be supposed to be of absorbing interest to a lady living in seclusion.

The cards, which have a diameter of $1\frac{1}{2}$ to $4\frac{1}{2}$ inches, are divided into eight or ten suits, each composed of ten numeral cards and two courts, and illustrate the *Avatâras*, or incarnations, of Vishnu, the second god in the Hindu Trinity, the other two being Brahma and Siva. Vishnu is regarded by his devotees as the source of the universe and all other gods are believed to be but differing aspects or emanations of him. He sleeps in the primaeval ocean on the thousand-headed snake Sesa.

The Vaisnavite believes in ten incarnations, in the first three of which Vishnu appeared as a wonderful animal, for example a golden fish with a horn 10,000 miles long, and in the next six in human form. The seventh is yet to come. In each case his purpose was either to remedy a moral or religious wrong or destroy influence hostile to the Brahmanic caste.

It is not claimed that European cards are directly descended from Indian cards, nor could it be since there is not the slightest resemblance between the two. But it is argued that European cards have an Indian lineage on the grounds that two Hindu gods flourish symbols remarkably like those of early European cards. *Hanumant,* the monkey god, one of the heroes of the seventh *Avatâr,* holds in four of his hands a cup, a sword, a ring and a sceptre; *Ardhanârisvâra,* meaning 'half-female lord', who is a figure half Siva and half his bride Devi holds a cup, a sword, a coin and a baton in his and her hands. The early European suits were cups, swords, coins and batons.

A third claimant to the parentage of European cards is found in Persia. Usually about $2\frac{1}{2} \times 1\frac{3}{4}$ inches, the faces of old Persian cards have figures of women, youths, dancing-girls, lions eating serpents, kings and queens on thrones and other like designs upon a green, yellow, black, red or golden background. Sometimes the cards were made of ivory and sometimes of lacquered paper. And Dr Culin remarks, 'from travellers in the seventeenth century we know that a set of *Ganjifa* consisted of 90 or 96 cards in 8 suits or colours'. *Ganjifa* was one game played by the Persians; another was *âs-nâs,* from which gin rummy, poker and all other games based on the same principle are descended. Persian cards bear no more resemblance to European cards than do Chinese or Indian, their claim to ancestry resting solely on *âs-nâs* being the forerunner of so many of our games of chance.

If it be accepted that the suit marks of European cards have been copied from the symbols of a four-handed Hindu god, or from the signs on Chinese cards, or that European cards have a Persian ancestry, then the question arises 'How were these symbols brought to the notice of an Italian Renaissance painter?' Several answers have been given. The first, 'brought by the gipsies', held that these wandering folk, who had their origins somewhere in India, brought oriental cards and carvings with them in their migration westwards. This theory is no longer tenable since it is now known that cards were established in Europe before the gipsy advance-guard reached the eastern approaches. The second and third answers are two sides of the same coin. Both sides agree that cards and carvings travelled along the great Peking to Samarkand silk routes, in caravans of thousands of camels (4700 is the largest chronicled) jostling silks and spices, soap and sugar, rose water and rhinoceros horns, vermilion dyes, kapok and much else. From Samarkand they were taken, by more conventional systems of trade and travel, through Persia to Syria and the Holy Land, whence they were carried into Europe either by the Saracens or the Crusaders.

12

Early Indian playing cards. Collection R. Tilley

Nine cards from a modern Japanese *Flower Game*. Each card is one of four representing each of the twelve months: here *(from left to right)* plum blossom (second month), eularia (eighth month), maple (tenth month), peony (sixth month), pine (first month), iris (fifth month), willow (eleventh month), chrysanthemum (ninth month) and wisteria (fourth month). The other months are represented by cherry blossom, clover and paulownia. Collection Evelyn Goshawk; photo Peter Kibbles

The Saracenic school of thought points out that the Saracens, Moors or Arabs, names which were interchangeable, occupied the whole of North Africa, from Egypt to the Atlantic, as well as Spain. Being highly cultivated—they led Europe in mathematics and philosophy—as well as widely spread, they were advantageously placed to penetrate a variety of European countries and introduce playing cards. And that they took advantage of their opportunities, the claim continues, is shown by the similarity between the Arabic word for cards, *naib,* and the Spanish *naipes*. M. L'Abbé Rive in his *Ecclairissements Historiques et Critiques sur l'Invention des Cartes à Jouer* goes a step further and actually names the inventor. He says: '1330. On les voit en Espagne vers cette année, et bien long-temps qu'on trouve la moindre trace dans aucune autre nation. Elles y ont été inventées par un nommé Nicolao Pepin.' He goes on to explain that the word *naipes* is derived from Señor Pepin's initials. A fascinating account of the life of another suggested inventor is given by J. Ant. Pellicer in a note to his life of Cervantes:

The ironical manner in which the author here speaks of the origins of cards is plainly seen. Of the same stock, and from the same source, came that theory which was current in the seventeenth century, among the Andalusian gamesters. Respecting the inventor of cards who was supposed to be a certain countryman, there were three opinions. Some said that he was a Frenchman, because the first cards came from France into Spain; others that he was a Fleming, on account of the invention of the game of Cent by the ladies of Flanders; and others that he was a native of Madrid, and that having there lost his all, he took his

way toward Seville, with an intention of seeing that city. At Orgaz, a place in the kingdom of Toledo, he learned and exercised the trade of a mason, where, in memory of his occupation he built a famous chimney; he was afterward waiter at an inn at Sierra Morena, but some extraordinary accidents which befell him obliged him to seek service in Penaflor as a lamplighter, from whence he passed to Seville. After having become a sword-cutler, he died there, being burnt for coining. This was the father and inventor of cards, according to apocryphal memoirs of the gamblers, who often curse and renounce him.

However, strong though the case for the Arabs and Spain may be, there is an even stronger one for the Crusaders. Although they did little to advance the Christian cause, the Crusaders did much to benefit European society. In the course of two centuries, hundreds and thousands of men, accompanied in some cases by women, set out for the Holy Land. They came from all over the West. The widespread appeal of the call 'Deus Vult' was stressed by William of Malmesbury, the Anglo-Norman chronicler of the twelfth century. 'The most distant lands', he writes, 'were inspired by this ardent passion. The Welshman left his hunting, the Scotsman his fellowship with vermin, the Dane his drinking party, the Norwegian his raw fish.' The first bands of armed pilgrims, led by the colourful and valiant Walter the Pennyless and Peter the Hermit, travelled overland in tumultuous hordes. Later armies journeyed by sea, leaving vast profits in the coffers of the Mediterranean shipowners, notably those of Venice and Genoa. Although the expenditure of human life in the Holy Land itself was immense, many Crusaders lived to return to their native lands; and they, and the crews of the returning vessels, took back with them a new awareness of Greek and Saracenic culture, an appreciation of eastern wealth and refinement, and a reappraisal (for the worse) of papal policy. Their ships were filled with new commodities such as sugar, saddles and salves, cotton and, it is suggested, knapsacks stuffed with playing cards. If the original premise, that cards were available in the Holy Land, be accepted, then the case for their introduction into Europe being due to the Crusaders is a powerful one.

We now turn to two ideas concerning the origin of playing cards which are basically different from those already put forward, since they are grounded neither on a similarity of symbols nor a correspondence between games. The first notion is that dice fathered cards, the second that the same office was performed by chess. Dice can be given short shrift since the sole argument in their favour is the precise agreement between the possible number of throws in a set of three dice and the number of cards in the first European packs—fifty-six respectively. The case for chess is not much stronger, since the main contention is that in its original form (the ancient Indian game of *chaturanga*) it was played by four players, two against two, as were many western games. In its progress from east to west chess passed through several forms, and some significance may attach to the refusal of the Arabs and Persians to allow a woman to appear upon the board. They substituted a vizier for the queen. We have already noticed the likeness between the Spanish and Arabic words for cards, and we may now note that the Spanish never allowed a woman to appear in their packs. The queen was replaced by a *caballero*. But legend and guesswork and recondite reconstruction with their strange, siren spell can lead into a maze of unprofitable speculation. However well argued any of the foregoing ideas may be, none is entirely convincing, and none is supported by the authority of a single playing card. Even if it be allowed that eastern cards were invented in the harem or were derived from the Korean divinatory arrow, there is still nothing to prove that European cards were based on eastern. In the absence of such proof let us declare, until proved wrong, that European cards were invented by a European, adding the rider that it is possible that he drew his inspiration in the first place from the sight of an oriental pack or of a Hindu god.

2

The Renaissance and the first appearance of cards in Europe

Turning our backs on imitations of an imperial ancestry, we prepare to accept a less noble lineage. If the blood be not so blue as had been hoped, at least the period into which European cards were born, that of the Italian Renaissance, was one of unquestioned brilliance. And the foremost figures in the early years of the Renaissance, and also in the first annals of playing cards, was Francesco Petrarch, who was born in 1304 and died in 1375. For in the passage from the mediaeval to the modern world Petrarch foreshadows the beginning of the modern, and it was Petrarch who gave the initial impulse to the study of Latin literature, which, in its turn, inspired a thirst for Greek.

In card history Petrarch is important in a purely negative way, in that it seems that despite a long life and extensive travels he never so much as caught a glimpse of a pack of playing cards. Had he done so, surely he would have mentioned the matter somewhere in his copious writings, which did not overlook dice and gambling. A like omission is true, also, of his friend and contemporary Boccaccio who would undoubtedly have written of cards in *The Decameron* had he ever seen them. Similarly negative, neither of two prescriptions of other games, one, dated 1363, being an ordinance issued by the Church strictly prohibiting certain clerics from playing at dice or taking part in games of chance, and one, dated 1369, being an edict by Charles V of France, forbidding sports and pastimes by name, makes any mention of cards.

Fortunately we have several positives to offset the negatives, and the two fit together as neatly as the tenons and mortises of a dovetail joint. The earliest is the Greek influence which spread throughout Italy, the promptings of which can be seen in the trumps of the tarot; but the most important is a sermon composed by a German monk who lived in the ancient city of Basle, one of the great, if not the greatest, literary centres of the time. In his sermon the monk, who gives his name as Johannes, states quite clearly that 'the game of cards has come to us this year, viz the year of our Lord MCCCLXXVII', and since the original manuscript is in the possession of the British Museum, where it can be seen by anyone with the necessary authority, the evidence is difficult to deny. Furthermore, there immediately follows a whole range of other positives, such as prohibitions by John of Castile, and in the cities of Florence and Basle itself in the self-same year, by the city of Regensburg or Ratisbon, one of the oldest cities in Germany, in 1378, and by an entry in the accounts of the Duchy of Brabant in 1379, to name but some. With the dates coming together so comfortably there seems little reason to doubt that cards first appeared in

Europe at some time in the second half of the fourteenth century.

There are other documents which give, or appear to give, earlier dates for this important birthday; but none of them is an original manuscript, and in each case it is thought that the mention of cards, or the date given for their first appearance, has been added by a later hand. Alterations, additions and interpolations by a later editor who either thought that the original author had made a mistake, or by mischance had left something out, or wished to foist some opinion of his own upon an unsuspecting public. In card history documents suspected of having been so amended are three French manuscripts, *Renard le Contrefait* by an anonymous author and thought to have been written between 1328 and 1341; the *Histoire et Chronique de Provence par Cesar Nostradamus*, published in Lyons in 1614 and in which cards appear about 1361; and Antoine de la Salle's *Chronique de Petit Jehan le Saintre* written in the reign of Charles V: a German treatise *Das Guldin Spil* printed in Augsburg in 1472 in which the author, a Dominican monk called Johann Ingold, writes 'ich gelesan han, so ist es gekommen in teutschland der ersten, in dem jar, da man zait von crist geburt tausend dreihundert jar', which is to say that the author has read that cards were introduced into Germany in the year 1300: and a manuscript *Trattato del Giverno della Famiglia* written in 1299 by Pipoza di Sandro of Florence but since lost except for a mention in the work of the eighteenth-century Italian literary historian Tiraboschi. A somewhat different piece of misleading 'evidence' is a miniature in a work which can be shown to have been written between 1371 and 1373. In the illustration two ladies wearing steeple-headdresses and a young man wearing a small cap and long hair are shown playing at cards. But the fashions are undoubtedly nearer 1470 than 1370, and the document cannot, therefore, be accepted as proof that cards were known in, or before, 1371.

Returning to the sermon, Johannes of Basle speaks of kings sitting on royal thrones, each supported by two *marschalli* and of queens, each with two attendants. Alas! there is no description of the attendants, who, presumably, were female and either ladies-in-waiting or ladies-of-the-bed-chamber. They must have brightened the pack; but they have disappeared from the royal retinue, leaving neither trace nor trail. The worthy friar mentions six different packs, ranging from fifty-two to sixty cards, each with ten numeral cards and with varying court cards; but he is so taken up with the composition of a splendid, moralizing sermon that he forgets to give any further account of the court cards or any at all of the suit signs, though he does remark that symbols appear on each of the cards. We can only guess that the signs were those traditional to Italy, namely cups (*coppe*), swords (*spade*), money (*denari*) and clubs (*bastoni*).

We have yet more speculation in front of us. The first question to which it must be applied is 'Where in Europe did western cards originate?' Clearly not Switzerland, since Johannes specifically states that they came into that country, leaving a choice to be made from other European countries by means of a reasoned guess.

The great resurgence of art during the Renaissance was not confined to any one field and included manuscript illumination and miniature painting. The latter, which reached its zenith during the fourteenth century, grew out of the former, continued with its techniques, and produced tiny, exquisite and faithful portraits; and as enthroned monarchs and mounted marshals are perfectly suitable subjects for the brush of the miniature painter it is reasonable to suppose that the first cards were the work of a miniaturist. Since the Renaissance first manifested itself in Italy, where schools of painting, with subsidiary schools of manuscript illumination and miniature painting were associated with the luxurious courts of Milan, Cremona, Verona, Ferrara and elsewhere, and since the ducal families of those cities, the Visconti, Sforza and Este were, Charles VI of France apart, the earliest card owners of whom we know, it seems sensible to guess that the unknown miniaturist was an Italian working in the northern part of his country.

How did this miniaturist come to paint a pack of cards? Maybe the painter's idea was prompted by the sight of an oriental pack; but it is much more likely that his point of departure was a commission to portray the ruling family in a series of miniatures. At that time these little portraits were in much demand among the wealthy classes for wedding presents and keepsakes, and to some extent they served the same purpose as the modern family photo-album. This custom would seem to provide the sort of familiar activity out of which a game might develop in the manner suggested in the discussion of oriental cards. On the whole a possible solution to the problem is that it occurred to the artist to devise some visual aids to teaching—possibly using, in the first place, drawings or paintings which failed for some reason or other to reach the standard required for the ducal commission which would otherwise have been wasted.

A need for such aids must have arisen out of the tremendous revival of education following on the upsurge of learning. The Renaissance was one of the greatest periods in the history of education. And if our 'golden guess is morning-star to the full round of truth', as Tennyson puts it, there would have been nothing particularly original in such a scheme. What else are stained-glass windows, the Stations of the Cross, holy statues and paintings of the saints if they are not visual aids to teaching religious knowledge? Did not St John of Damascus write as early as the eighth century, "if I have no books I go to church"? This, too, was the intention of the mediaeval bestiary or physiologue. In *An English Thirteenth-Century Bestiary*, the authors say 'in some codices Book I is preceded by a letter' and 'in this letter Hugo states that he has decided to paint a picture of a dove' with 'wings covered with silver and the hinder parts of her back with the paleness of gold' (c.f. Psalm LXVII Douay version). This, he states, he does with intent 'to instruct the illiterate with pictures, and thus seek to convey the spiritual allegory graphically to minds incapable of comprehending philosophic concepts'.

In the case of a pack of cards instructive or moralizing stories could have been woven round the sixteen court cards, while the numbered cards could have been ideal for elementary instruction in cyphering. The symbols themselves, chalices or cups, coins, swords and batons, could have been used as the basis of lessons on the Eucharist in the first case, or the love of money being the root of all evil in the second, and so on. The stroke of genius lay in devising such aids as were capable of being used for games, so that much scholarship could be absorbed subliminally while the pupil was engaged in a pleasant pastime. And it is interesting that Sir William Wilkinson includes in his report on Chinese cards the following passage: 'Cards based on a writing lesson. The earliest, or one of the earliest, writing lessons set to a Chinese child is "Once [there was] a great man".'

3

The tarot

The first packs of which we have individual knowledge are three painted for Charles VI, King of France, in 1392, total information being limited to a record in the accounts of the royal treasurer, M. Charles Poupart. The entry reads 'Donné à Jacquemin Gringonneur, peintre, pour trois jeux de cartes à or, et à diverses couleurs, ornés de plusieurs devises, pour porter à Seigneur Roi, pour son ébatement LVI sols Parisis.' No other description of the cards is given, but seventeen cards in the Cabinet des Estampes of the Bibliothèque Nationale in Paris have been claimed as survivors of the three packs. Painted in gesso and body colour on a golden field with a silver border and with as many devices as there are cards, they are in harmony with the accounting entry; nevertheless it is generally thought that they are fifteenth-century copies rather than late-fourteenth-century originals. They show the influence of Italian painting, which carries no surprise in view of the many French contacts with Italian culture. Charles VI came of a family of great patrons of art and literature. His father, Charles V called the Wise, had a passion for architecture and the laying out of gardens, and extended enthusiastic patronage to the miniaturists. Charles V's brother, John, duc de Berry, assembled collections somewhat smaller than those of the king but formed with greater care and taste. So it was with other members of the family, and so it was, presumably, with Charles VI, from which we may fairly conclude that he ordered the three packs of beautifully painted and richly ornamented cards in order to satisfy his personal delight in all 'good, subtle and beautiful things', as was said of Louis II de Bourbon.

Assuming that the seventeen cards in the Bibliothèque Nationale are either survivors, or true copies, of those painted for Charles VI, then His Majesty's packs had one, at the very least, tremendous difference from those described in the sermon of 1377. For those cards of Charles VI are of a kind unmentioned by, and presumably unknown to, Johannes, in his sermon, being a type known in French as *atouts* or tarots, and in Italian as *attuti* or *trionfi* or *tarocchi*, because they triumph over, or are superior to, all others. Their full number is twenty-two, and with the fifty-six other cards they make up a tarot pack, sometimes referred to as 'the tarot'. In play they were used for the complicated game of *tarocchi*, once extremely popular in northern Italy, where we have guessed that they were invented, and southern France, moderately popular in Hungary, scarcely known elsewhere, and completely unknown in Spain. For a long time now they have appeared more often in the fortune-teller's booth than on the card table. The fifty-six

See colour illustration page 37

other cards are divided into four suits of fourteen cards each, consisting of numeral cards one to ten and four court cards named in Italian *Re*, *Regina*, *Cavallo* and *Fante*, or king, queen, knight and knave (the queen is excluded from the ordinary pack). The suit signs, again in Italian, are *coppe* (cups or chalices), *spade* (swords), *denari* (coins) and *bastoni* (batons). The swords are curved and the batons straight, and both are bundled together with, very often, interleaving or plaiting. The kings are always seated with their legs crossed. The cards tend to be long and narrow and the backs have a small, simple pattern and the paper is folded over the face making a narrow border and affording some protection to the edges.

Some scholars have claimed that the inventor of playing cards deliberately chose the suit symbols for philosophic reasons, the intention being to illustrate either four of the virtues or the four classes into which mediaeval society was divided. If he were devising some visual aids to teaching, as we have supposed, the scholars may well have been right. The allusions are said to be, in the first case, to the sword of Justice, the club of Fortitude, the coin of Charity and the cup of Faith, and in the second to the Eucharistic cups or chalices of the Church, the swords of the military, the coins of the merchants and the clubs of the peasants.

When we examine the sequence of twenty-two trumps, of which the seventeen of Charles VI are part, we are confronted with the greatest problem in card history, one which has caused more books to be written than the whole of the rest of the subject put together. Even less is certainly known of the origins of the trumps of ordinary cards. Though they are not heard of for fifteen years after other cards, accepting that Charles VI's cards were tarot packs, or about eighty years if we wait for the first unequivocal documentary evidence, many writers have claimed on the most nebulous grounds that the tarot dates back to the remote past. The strange, haunting faces of the cards are, apparently, allusive, and in consequence endless efforts have been made to discover their meaning.

It seems alas that interpreting the tarot has more often been the employment of vendors of the pseudo-occult than the subject of serious scholarship. 'I am rather inclined to the opinion', says one author, when speaking of the sixth card, the Lovers, 'that it represents the Qabalistic Microprosopus between Binah and Maikuth, while the figure above shows the Influence descending from Kether', to which it is very difficult for the ordinary reader to attach any meaning whatsoever.

A different example of uninformed speculation is to be found in the tracing back of the word tarot to the ancient Egyptian *Tar*, meaning road, and *Ro* or *Rog* or *Ros* meaning royal, and then interpreting the whole as the Royal Road to Salvation.

The trumps, with their names printed at the foot of the face of each card, more often in French than in Italian, are: I *Le Bateleur* or *Il*

See colour illustrations
pages 40, 41

Bagatto (the Juggler or the Sorcerer); II *La Papesse* or *La Papessa* (the Popess); III *L'Imperatrice* (the Empress); IV *L'Empereur* or *L'Imperatore* (the Emperor); V *Le Pape* or *Il Papa* (the Pope); VI *L'Amoureux* or *Gli Amanti* (the Lovers); VII *Le Chariot* or *La Carossa* (the Chariot); VIII *La Justice* or *La Giustizia* (Justice); IX *L'Ermite* or *L'Eremita* (the Hermit); X *La Roue de Fortune* or *Ruota della Fortuna* (the Wheel of Fortune); XI *La Force* or *La Forza* (Force); XII *Le Pendu* or *L'Appeso* (the Hanging Man); XIII Usually unnamed, presumably for superstitious reasons, but clearly Death; XIV *La Temperance* or *La Temperanza* (Temperance); XV *Le Diable* or *Il Diavolo* (the Devil); XVI *La Maison de Dieu* or *La Torre* (the House of God or the Tower); XVII *L'Etoile* or *Le Stelle* (the Star); XVIII *La Lune* or *La Luna* (the Moon); XIX *Le Soleil* or *Il Sole* (the Sun); XX *Le Jugement* or *Il Giudizio* (Judgement); XXI *Le Monde* or *Il Mondo* (the World); and unnumbered *Le Fou* (or *Le Mat*) or *Il Matto* (the Fool).

These are the cards that are to be found in old packs in museums and big private collections and they correspond very well, if not precisely, with the list given in the earliest known documentary authority, a sermon which was the subject of a lecture by 'Robert Steele Esq. FSA read to the Society of Antiquaries, 31 May 1900, and reported in volume LVII of *Archaeologia*. Early in his lecture Mr Steele declared:

A manuscript volume of sermons, now in my possession, written circa 1450–70, contains a passage of some importance for the history of card games. It occurs in a sermon per utilis de ludo under the sub-heading Ludi Inductio, f. 208.

Ad cujus evidentiam queritur, quis invenit ludum? Respondeo quod tria sunt genera ludorum fortunae, viz. Taxillorum, Cartularum, et Triuphorum. . . . [For clarification of which the question is asked, 'Who invented gaming?' I answer that there are three kinds of games of chance, namely the dice, the cards and the trumps. . . .]

The careful separation of trumps and dice is of the first importance. The last two paragraphs of the sermon read:

Concerning the third class of games, that is trumps. There is nothing in the world so hateful to God as the game of trumps. For everything that is base in the eyes of the Christian faith is seen in trumps, as will be evident when I run through them. For trumps are said, so it is believed, to have been given their names by the Devil, their inventor, because in no other game does he triumph (with the loss of souls to boot) as much as in this one. In it not only are God, the angels, the planets and the cardinal virtues represented and named, but also the world's luminaries, I mean the Pope and the Emperor, are forced, a thing which is degrading and ridiculous to Christians, to enter into the game. For there are 21 trumps which are the 21 steps of a ladder which takes a man to the depths of Hell.

The sermon then proceeds to detail the trumps, and the list differs but slightly from that already mentioned. The order of cards differs in one or two places, the Popess, for instance, coming fourth instead of second. Death is named. The Juggler is called the Mountebank, the Hermit the Hunchback, the Maison de Dieu the Arrow, and Judgement the Angel.

Maybe there are small variations in order and name. The reference to God, the angels, the planets and the cardinal virtues is obscure. The derived game of *minchiate,* first heard of in 1415 and dealt with in chapter 4, has forty-one trumps, a number reached by the addition of the three Theological Virtues, Prudence, the four Elements, and the twelve signs of the Zodiac. Some of the asides are unintelligible. Nevertheless there is no doubt as to which cards the author of the sermon is referring, and the 'importance of this notice', as Mr Steele points out in the final paragraph of his lecture, 'is that it shows that the game of triumphs was recognized as distinct from games of cards, and ranked with dice and cards as a division of gaming'.

It seems evident that the trump cards came into being separately from ordinary cards, and equally evident, since they are not heard of until some years after the others, that they were invented, or evolved, at a later date. And this obviousness is powerfully supported by internal indications, contained in the detail of the cards. The suggestion now made is that they were contrived at a time when several bands of heretics, who had taken refuge in the Italian valleys of the Cottian Alps, to the west of Milan, were being subjected to exceptional pressures by the Inquisition. The most important of these groups were the Waldenses, and for reasons advanced below they are now put forward as the possible originators of the trumps and the amalgamators of the two types of cards to form the basis of the game of *tarocchi.*

For the greater part of a thousand years the Cottian Alps formed a refuge to many 'distressed' and 'discontented' people who, being in opposition to Rome, were liable to persecution at the dictates of the established Church. Probably the first to find refuge in the remote valleys were the followers of Claude, Bishop of Turin, who went about his diocese tearing down the crosses and crucifixes so beloved of the Church of Rome, while instructing his flock that 'If people wish to adore a cross because Christ hung upon it, they ought also to adore mangers because He lay in one, or asses because He rode on one.' In the fifteenth century, while Charles VI of France was enjoying the beauty of his specially painted cards, the valleys were sheltering the remnants of seventeen different sects. Of these the most important were the Waldenses, who in time absorbed most, if not all, of the others who were excommunicated by Lucian III in 1183.

The curse pronounced by Roman ecclesiastical authority automatically banned heretics from the Church, denied them the Sacraments which were held to be essential to eternal life, and forbade absolutely any association with other Christians.

The Waldensian ministers were commonly known as *barbe*, plural of *barba*, meaning 'uncle'. All *barbe* were required to take their turn as missionaries. They marched out of the valleys, two by two in the true Biblical style, braving, and often suffering, martyrdom in their constant search for converts. Italy, and in particular Lombardy in the north, was their main field of endeavour. There are interesting stories of missionaries travelling south through Genoa, Pisa, Florence, Rome and Naples to Calabria, and then returning along the Adriatic coast by way of Brindisi, Ancona, Venice and Milan. Others went over the Alps into Germany, Bohemia, Austria, Poland and even Bulgaria. Besides seeking converts they visited, comforted and strengthened the faithful, who could not openly avow their faith.

The successful dissemination of Waldensian principles was not achieved without unflinching heroism, iron resolution and fixity of purpose.

In view of the appalling treatment to which the *barbe* were liable, it is no surprise to read that they travelled in disguise. Indeed, with the Inquisition keeping a sharp look out for fresh victims it would have been impossible for them to have stirred from the valleys unless their true vocation were hidden. Inquisitor Stephen de Borbonne testifies:

'It happened sometimes that one of their chiefs was imprisoned who had in his possession many disguises, with which he assumed different forms like Prometheus. . . . Now he had the dress and usual attire of a pilgrim; now he had the fictitious habit of a shoemaker, now of a barber, now of a mower.'

It would have been equally impossible to take with them a copy of their own instructional material. Yet without pictures the meaning of which could be grasped clearly by anyone, however scant their learning—how could the *barbe,* or anyone else for that matter, set about the task of education? Therefore we can believe that they disguised their illustrations as well as their persons, and it follows that the disguise must have taken the form of something easily explained away to an inquisitive official. Could anything serve this purpose better than a pack of cards? Would that have been so very different from the paper-makers who, according to Harold Bayley in his books *The Lost Language of Symbolism* and *A New Light on the Renaissance*, had the happy thought of sending 'signals of hope and encouragement to their fellow exiles in far distant countries' by means of water-marks? How else can one explain the remark of the American scholar Henry Charles Lea in his *History of the Inquisition* that 'everywhere they [the *barbe*] met friends acquainted with their secret passwords, and in spite of ecclesiastical vigilance there existed throughout Italy a subterranean network of heresy disguised under outward conformity'?

The symbolism of the twenty-two trump cards must, therefore, be examined in detail to assess their hidden meaning for these scattered converts to the reformed faith.

Trump No I Le Bateleur *Le Bateleur* generally appears as a man in motley standing behind a table on which are a number of small articles difficult to identify. With his left hand he holds aloft a short rod, presumably a magician's wand, while in his right hand he clasps a ball which, at a guess, he is on the point of making disappear. Sometimes he has a last and other tools of the cobbler's trade set out before him. The title is variously translated by writers on the tarot as the Mountebank, the Juggler, the Sorcerer and, occasionally, the Cobbler.

We have the evidence of two inquisitors that the *barbe* included in their disguises the role of a cobbler. We have the authority of yet a third inquisitor, Reinerus Saccho, a turncoat heretic, that the pastors roved the countryside disguised as pedlars. These contemporary records show clearly and convincingly that *Le Bateleur* could have represented a *barba*. In the hands of one of the faithful, perhaps far from sanctuary and surrounded by religious enemies, the sight of the card must have brought great encouragement and stiffening of resistance. In the hands of a *barba* the card may have been used as a sort of passport, a *carte d'identité*, an introduction to the faithful and a certificate that the bearer would not betray his contacts to the Holy Office.

Trump No II La Papesse *La Papesse* is generally translated as the High Priestess for the simple reason that a genuine female pope has never been known and some other wording must, therefore, be found. She is shown seated, clothed in impressive robes, and normally wearing a beeskip head-dress modelled on the papal crown and encircled usually by two, occasionally by one or three, diadems. Now and again she wears a crown by itself.

There can be little doubt that the words *La Papesse* were intended to mean the female pope, or the popess, and that the picture was designed, in the first place, as a representation of Pope Joan: for the legend of the female pope was firmly believed until the fifteenth century brought new canons of criticism. Only then was doubt cast upon the story of the daughter of an English missionary in Germany who, through her genius for learning and pretended piety, was elevated to the papal throne as John VII, who then admitted a member of her household to her bed, and who was delivered of a son at a point between the Coliseum and St Clement's Church in Rome during the course of a solemn Whitsun procession through the streets of Rome in the company of her clergy.

The Popess follows *Le Bateleur* as naturally as a cardboard queen

Cavalier de l'Epée from a French
tarot pack by J. Jerger, *c.* 1800.
Bowes Museum, Durham

Le Bateleur from a French tarot
pack by J. Jerger, *c.* 1800.
Bowes Museum, Durham

follows a cardboard king. A priest disguised as a cobbler is followed by a harlot disguised as a priest. This card could be interpreted as Babylon of the Book of Revelation.

Trumps Nos III and IV   L'Imperatrice and L'Empereur   Both Empress and Emperor are shown enthroned. Each holds in one hand a sceptre, tipped with an orb. The Empress has a shield, normally charged with an eagle, in her right hand, and the Emperor a similar shield, with like device, on the ground by his left foot. Because of the manner in which it soars above the earth, the eagle was the accepted symbol of empire and dominion. The Empress has an ordinary sort of crown, but the Emperor's head-dress provides a small pointer towards the date of origin of the trumps. Shaped something like a coal scuttle, it appears to be an adaptation of a *salade* or *sallet*.

These two cards follow the last as naturally as one porpoise follows another. The Popess, with picture of a wanton, drew attention to the immorality prevailing in Church and Society. The Emperor and Empress picture a lawfully wedded couple and symbolize the Waldensian teaching on marriage. The high rank of the wife, equal to that of her husband, points to the sect's belief that the religious standing of a good woman matched that of a good man. At a time when life lived singly in absolute continence and virginity was commonly held to be the ideal, and wedlock, though necessary for the continuance of the race, to be in some way inferior, the Waldenses upheld the married state.

Trump No V   Le Pape   The Pope is portrayed sitting on his throne, clothed in heavy, impressive robes, on his head the beehive head-dress with three coronets, in his left hand a sceptre surmounted by a triple cross and on his hands gloves with Maltese crosses on the backs. Three tonsured figures kneel before him and his raised right hand, with two fingers outstretched, suggests that the acolytes are receiving a blessing. The triple crown is of great importance, since the third coronet, as already noted, was only added in 1315 or 1316. In consequence it is difficult to see how the tarot can antedate the year 1315, let alone stretch back to remote antiquity as is sometimes maintained.

This card offers texts for some of the most treasured articles of the Waldensian faith. In the first place, it was cardinal to their teaching that they rejected the supremacy of the Pope, boldly declaring that while the Church of Rome was originally the true Church she had been seduced by Constantine's Donation, and by consenting to be endowed by the state had become morally corrupt.

The Waldenses not only rallied against the Church for being led astray by worldly power, dominion and wealth but protested against all religious endowments of any nature whatsoever and any temporal powers of the clergy.

Le Chariot from a French tarot pack by J. Jerger, *c.* 1800. Bowes Museum, Durham

Finally, the Waldenses were opposed to all vestments and personal adornment, to the use of crosses, images and ornaments in churches, all benedictions and the tonsure, all of which are well illustrated in the card, and all ecclesiastical customs not expressly authorized by the scriptures.

Trump No VI L'Amoureux The sixth card portrays a young man in doublet and hose standing between two women, one richly dressed and wearing a laurel wreath and the other soberly clad. Cupid, apparently about to let fly an arrow already fitted to his bow, hovers above the trio.

This card points to one of the fundamental beliefs of the Waldenses, namely that one cannot serve God and Mammon and must choose between Love of God and Love of Possessions. The Love of Possessions decked out in splendid clothes outshines the Love of God in the garments of humility. Her laurel wreath, in the heroic past the emblem of victory wound round the head of conquering heroes, would appear to have been self-awarded, since the next card makes it clear that the young man made the correct choice.

The final interpretation of this card may be yet more profound, for the choice between things temporal and things spiritual implies a deeper selection, that between good and evil.

That the young man should be clad in doublet and hose is a small detail of large importance, for it was not until the second quarter of the fourteenth century that the ankle length tunic began to be shortened. By about 1335 the doublet had established itself and male legs were much in evidence.

Trump No VII Le Chariot In this card we are shown a young man riding in a rectangular vehicle the body of which is set high above the wheels. He is crowned and wearing a metal breast plate ornamented with pauldrons, or embossed shoulder pieces, each of which is designed as a human face looking upwards and outwards. In his right hand he carries a long arrow or wand of authority. The chariot is drawn by a pair of horses, normally joined together at the rump, but often without hind legs, and generally without bridle or reins. Four painted pillars, one at each corner, support a canopy.

In its simplest form the lesson of this card follows quite naturally upon that of the last, for this is clearly a triumphal chariot and teaches that the right choice made at the decisive moment illustrated in the previous card results in a man's whole nature being changed and in his becoming poised to make a triumphal journey along the road to salvation.

In ancient times the horse was the symbol of the haste with which a man ought to race towards the Gospel, the Good News, by which alone his salvation could be assured. Nothing in this picture detracts from that truth.

30

Can it be coincidence that the seventh trump was chosen for the card illustrating a young man on the road to salvation? Surely there is a relation between the card and the science of numerology. The number 7, being compounded of 3, representing the Trinity and all things spiritual, and 4, the number of the elements and therefore of all things material, was long regarded as symbolic of man's dual nature.

That the momentous nature of its symbolism was accepted by the Holy Fathers, as well as by the Church, is shown by their formulation into groups of seven of a wide range of acts of spiritual significance: the seven Sacraments, the seven Cardinal Virtues, the seven Deadly Sins. In the circumstances it is hard to believe that mere chance led 'the Master of the Tarot' to equate the road to salvation with the number seven.

Two very interesting pointers to the date of the original designs occur in this card. The first of these is the type of vehicle. For a long time chariots consisted simply of a seat which was open to the front and without any covering overhead, always excepting the Roman matron's *carpentum*, which had a canopy. The covered chariot, or wagon, came into use in France towards the end of the fourteenth century, and gave way to the carriage—a vehicle with a suspended body—at the end of the fifteenth, or the beginning of the sixteenth century.

The second pointer is provided by the pauldrons. Embossed designs on armour were directly contrary to good craftsmanship. They not only destroyed the 'glancing surface' but presented a protuberance in which the point or edge of an enemy's sword could catch, thereby retaining the full force of the blow and hindering the free movement of the metal plates from which the armour was made. But the important point is that pauldrons did not come into fashion until the fifteenth century, making yet another design detail pointing to that period as seeing the birth of the tarot.

Trump No VIII   La Justice   The unusual feature of this card is that it is entirely usual. It has a completely conventional design. Justice is depicted as a woman seated on a throne with a double-edged sword in her right hand and scales in her left. Her eyes are uncovered indicating heavenly justice, which is all-seeing, rather than earthly justice which, since it can discern but little, is normally shown blindfold.

Trump No IX   L'Ermite   The figure on this card is that of an old man dressed in a brown, monkish robe, with a staff in his left hand and a lantern, held up so as to light his way, in his right. In some old packs this figure has a pointed hood hanging from the robe, when the card is entitled *Le Capuchin*.

It cannot be seriously doubted that this drawing represents St Antony the Great. But here the *barbe* seem to have had a multi-purpose card, for it could be used for telling the life story of Peter Waldo, the

Founder of the sect. Both Peter Waldo and St Antony renounced their worldly goods, distributing among the poor what remained of extensive property, St Antony withdrawing into the desert to practise those austerities for which he is renowned and Peter Waldo tramping the countryside preaching and living on the alms of those who listened to him.

Trump No X   La Roue de Fortune   This trump depicts a free-standing wheel with a trio of peculiar creatures set about it. On the right-hand side, being whirled aloft, is an animal resembling a fox but with a lion's tufted tail in place of a brush. On the left, tumbling down, is a creature with a human face and, also, a lion-like tail. Above, crouched on a platform, is a third animal, winged, crowned and holding a sword. Sometimes, instead of the falling animal there is an urn, of the kind anciently used for the casting of lots, with smoke or flames rising from it. It stands on a pedestal, beside the base of which there is a human face. Sometimes the rising animal clings to the rim of the wheel and sometimes it sits on a spoke; sometimes it has claws.

The Wheel of Fortune taught mediaeval man that ups and downs are inherent in life, that the rich man of today is the poor man of tomorrow, and that pride precedes a fall and 'whosoever exalteth himself shall be abased, and that he that humbleth himself shall be exalted', that God alone is immutable and on Him our attention should be fixed. The urn, when present, makes the additional point that every effort should be made to ascertain the Divine Will, for the casting of lots was held to be a legitimate means of so doing.

Trump No XI   La Force   The eleventh trump depicts a woman standing beside a lion and holding its mouth agape. This feat appears to require neither greater courage nor bigger effort than a woman of today needs to open her purse. The woman, be it noted, has the crown of her hat formed, or sometimes encircled, by a crown of royalty; though as she has neither sceptre nor orb of queenship, evidently she is not of this world.

Since the card cannot, in the circumstances, refer to physical power it can only speak of spiritual or moral force. Spiritual courage and the force implicit in the faith that moves mountains are explicit in the woman's pose.

Trump Nos XII and XIII   Le Pendu and Le Mort (or unnamed)
The picture on the twelfth card is of a man hanging upside down from the crossbeam of a gallows to which he is secured by a narrow thong bound round his left ankle. His right leg is crossed behind his left and his hands are behind his back. He appears to be relaxed and happy in this curious position, and often smiles. There is no suggestion of torture or execution.

Death is clearly the motif of the thirteenth card although the

Chinese cards representing
(from left to right) bamboo,
prunus, orchid and
chrysanthemum, probably
early nineteenth century.
Slide collection Roger Tilley

designer usually yields to the timid by omitting the dread word. A gruesome figure of a skeleton, swinging a scythe, bestrides the card, and all around are heads and feet and hands which appear to be growing out of the ground and to be curiously alive, rather than lying inert as they would be if they had simply been shorn from their bodies.

These two cards, which follow neatly upon the previous one, must be read together. The narrow thong by which *Le Pendu* hangs indicates that his ties with this world are now but few and that he will soon come face to face with his neighbour Death. The promise of the resurrection of the body is held out in the second card, and foreshadows the new, ever-lasting life built upon the framework, or skeleton, of the old. Death is seen as a change rather than an end, as the beginning of a new life. These two cards teach the faithful the truth of St Paul's saying that 'to die is gain' and bid them share the Apostle's 'desire to depart, and be with Christ, which is far better' (Philippines I, 21 and 31). This was also the point of view of many of the early Christians who welcomed death whether it came on the cross or in the arena.

It is interesting that the cross, normally the sign of hope to a dying Christian which one would expect *Le Pendu* to be contemplating, or to be holding, in order to gain comfort, is never to be seen. The Waldenses not only never made the sign of the cross, but declared that 'they would venerate neither the very cross on which Christ hung, nor the crown of thorns'.

Trump No XIV   La Temperance   On this trump Temperance is represented by a winged female pouring a stream of liquid from one vase into another. Traditionally, the symbol of Temperance is a measuring device, and here she seems to be measuring out an ewer of liquid. A modern definition of this virtue is 'Habitual moderation in regard to the indulgence of the natural appetites and passions'. It is compounded of the lesser virtues of abstinence, chastity and modesty.

Abstinence refers to the restraint necessary in eating and drinking and is opposed to gluttony and drunkenness.

Modesty governs the more sober emotions and includes humility.

Of these various virtues an inquisitor remarked that the Waldenses 'are chaste and temperate in meat and drink. They do not seek taverns or dances or other vanities.'

Trump No XV   Le Diable   The Devil, with bat wings partially, sometimes wholly, open and long ears, stands upright upon a stool or mini-pedestal. Two small demons, complete with horns and tails, stand one on each side of the stool, facing inwards, and are chained, usually to the pedestal, sometimes to one another, occasionally to the Devil. The picture leaves no doubt that the demons are the Devil's 'creatures' and will do as they are bid by him.

Trump No XVI   La Maison de Dieu   The House of God appears

34

as a tall, narrow tower, with two, occasionally three, windows, which has been struck by a tongue of forked lightning. The presumption is that it is on the point of destruction. Two men are seen tumbling to the ground, though there is nothing to show whether they have fallen from one of the windows or from the battlements. The symbolism of this card is straightforward, for the Waldenses despised all church buildings, looking upon them as no better than barns and believing them to be just as productive of confusion, and as obstructive of prayer and meditation, as was the Tower of Babel (which, according to ancient Chaldean legend, was rent and overthrown by fire from heaven). It may have been their expectation that God would raze all churches, even as lightning (one of the accepted Christian symbols of divine power) shatters the pictured tower.

Trump No XVII L'Etoile In the foreground of this card a naked woman with long hair kneels beside a river and pours the contents of a pitcher, apparently just filled from the stream, on to the ground before her. From the skies above a constellation composed of seven stars grouped round a larger and more brilliant eighth, shines down upon the scene. To one side, beyond the river, is a tree which generally, though not always, has a bird perched upon the topmost branch.

This drawing is so full of symbolism that its message must necessarily be of special importance. In the art of the Middle Ages an otherwise unidentified river was assumed to be the Jordan which in turn was the accepted symbol of baptism. Stars were the recognized emblem of heaven. The bush with the bird is the 'Peridexion', a representation of the tree of life, the sweet fruits of which are eternal truths drawing to themselves the souls of mankind here typified by the birds. Nor is this all, for the branches of the 'Peridexion' so frighten the Devil that he fears to stand within their shade, with the result that the tree offers a sanctuary to the souls of the righteous. This highly symbolic tree is the fifty-fourth and final item in the Waldensian's very own *Physiologue*.

The particular importance of this trump is that it allegorizes one of the Sacraments—baptism. In addition the Waldenses believed that only natural, plain unadulterated water should be used for the rite of baptism.

Trump No XVIII La Lune In this card there is a picture of a moon, generally full but occasionally crescent, whose face gazes down upon two barking dogs which crouch beside a river. Two towers are discernible, though indistinctly, in the background. A crayfish, of all unlikely creatures, is shown superimposed upon the river, sometimes half above the river and half above the bank, but never gives the impression of having been in the water, or having emerged from it, or struggled out of it.

Symbolism, like true love, is unchanging, and the meaning of the

35

river in this card cannot differ from that of the river in the last. It necessarily represents the Jordan and stands for baptism. The two towers were commonly used to indicate the gates of heaven. Even though unknown in Christian symbolism, the crayfish is extremely interesting.

This trump follows quite naturally upon the last. It warns the faithful that while baptism is the name of the road that leads to the gates of heaven it is not of itself a panacea against evil. The baptised must still be on guard against those who, like the crayfish, lie in wait for the unwary. Moreover the Waldenses denounced constantly the plain-song of the Church of Rome and all ecclesiastical songs which they characterized as the 'barking of dogs', a 'Clamor infernalis'. Can such an attitude be better illustrated than by a pair of dogs baying at the moon?

Trump No XIX   Le Soleil   The sun, whose face when painted on playing cards is not much different from that of the moon, here shines upon two lightly clad boys who stand side by side in front of a wall, an arm around each other's waist.

The sun was accepted by the Christians of the Middle Ages as the most glorious work of the Creator, which he bestows upon all men, good and evil alike. Likewise it was a symbol of all that is beautiful in the next world. The boys stand for the faithful. Does not St Paul declare 'Ye are children of God by faith in Jesus Christ' (Galations 3:26)? That they have not yet ascended unto heaven is shown by the wall which to the 'symbol-reader' indicated matter as opposed to spirit.

Trump No XX   Le Jugement   This card depicts the upper half of an angel floating on a cloud. He is winged, has a halo, and is blowing a trumpet, the notes of which shower down upon, and spread over, the earth. Beneath are three figures who, in answer to the blast, clamber from the grave on this 'the day of the Lord'.

The belief that every soul shall appear before the bar of heavenly justice is repeatedly stated in the New Testament, particularly in the parables. That the Waldenses held that the baptised Christian could face this ordeal with confidence has been shown in the three previous cards.

Trump No XXI   Le Monde   A young woman, naked but for scant draperies, occupies the centre of the card. She holds a wand in her left hand and is surrounded by an elliptical laurel wreath. In each of the corners of the card can be seen one of the creatures of Revelations IV, 7, the upper half of the winged man being in the top left hand corner, the eagle in the top right, the calf in the bottom left and the lion in the bottom right.

Long before the advent of the Waldenses the four creatures were believed to represent the main events in the life of Christ, the winged man typifying the Incarnation, the calf the Passion, the lion the

38

Resurrection and the eagle the Ascension. Since the beginning of the fifth century they have also been held to represent the four Evangelists. The young woman, surrounded by a laurel wreath, stands for Truth naked and triumphant.

This, then, the last instructional card unmistakably reminds the beholder of the main features of the Christian story as told in the four Gospels, and proclaims that the truth will prevail against all prevarications and distortions.

The Unnumbered Trump   Le Fou   This, the unnumbered trump, is devoted to a man in the traditional parti-coloured clothes of the jester or court fool. With one hand he holds across his shoulder a stick with a bundle tied to its end; with the other he grasps a staff. With a dog bounding at his heels, the jester tramps the countryside. Though his worldly possessions are no more than can be tied in a bundle, he appears to be in good heart and quite contented.

During the Middle Ages the professional fool was a figure familiar to all grades and ranks of society. The fools were mainly drawn from the ranks of poets, musicians and philosophers.

This card begs the beholder to recognize the wisdom in the 'folly' of the fool. Unencumbered by worldly goods, a man should step out towards the goal, eyes fixed upon the splendour at the arch of the rainbow rather than the dross at the end. Above all, he must not seek reward but serve God with pure, disinterested love.

The Emperor's helmet, the Pope's head-covering, the Lover's doublet and hose and the Charioteer's pauldrons together provide convincing evidence that the trumps of the tarot could not have been designed before the fourteenth century. Were there but one anticipatory feature it might be dismissed as coincidence; but four coincidences in a series of only twenty-two drawings stretch belief to breaking point. At the other end of the time scale, acceptance of the legend of the Popess together with the picture in the seventh trump of a chariot rather than a carriage point to the cards having been drawn not later than the middle of the fifteenth century. Why, when there are so many indications that they first saw the light of day in the fifteenth century, are these strange pictures usually credited with an obscure and remote past? The answer appears to fall into three parts. Firstly, most authors writing about the tarot base their arguments on designs which cannot be found in old packs. Indeed, A. E. Waite, whose *Key to the Tarot* is a particularly well known work on the subject, frankly admits that the pack about which he writes contains alterations made by himself, and he claims that he thus provides 'a rectified and perfected pack'. Again a crescent moon often appears on the head of the Popess and this, while certainly giving an oriental tinge to the design, is not to be found in early packs. Secondly the *Cabbala* and the *Books of Thoth* have all the attractions of ancient mysteries, and as few people are acquainted with

over the page
Set of trumps by a Swiss family of card-makers by the name of Rochias, about 1790. Collection Evelyn Goshawk; photo Peter Kibbles

LE BATELEUR

LA PAPESE

L'IMPERATRISE

L'EMPEREUR

L'ERMITE

LA ROUE·DE·FORTUN

LA FORCE

LE PENDU

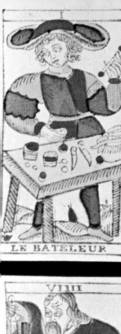

LES ETOILES

LA LUNE

LE SOLEIL

LE IUGEMENT

V

LE PAPE

VI

LAMOUREUX.

VII

LE CHARIOT

VIII

IUSTICE

XIII

LA MORT

XIIII

TEMPERANCE

XV

LE DIABLE

XVI

LA MAISON DE DIEU

XXI

LE MONDE

LE MAT

FAIT PAR JACQUES ROCHIAS FILS A NEUCHATEL

their teachings, and fewer still have the time or the opportunity or ability to read Latin or Greek versions, let alone the original texts, there is little difficulty in 'discovering' in them almost any dictum that suits an author's needs. For example, it is claimed that these works show that Egyptian priests were married and this is taken as sufficient justification for translating Papessa as High Priestess. Thirdly, the need to explain how the tarot migrated from east to west enables reference to be made to the gypsies. Surrounded by an aura compounded of mystery and romance, the gypsies automatically introduce a curious fascination into the tale. That there are serious flaws in any theory suggesting that the tarot was a Romany introduction into Europe appears to offer no

French tarot cards by Francois Bouvard. Bowes Museum, Durham

French tarot cards by J. Jerger, *c.* 1800. Bowes Museum, Durham

Cards from an Italian
minchiate pack, engraved on
steel and hand-painted, *c.* 1750.
Roger Tilley slide collection

Opposite
Nine cards from the *Book of
Trades* by Jost Ammon. Suits
are books, printers' pads,
wine-pots and drinking cups.
Staatliche Kunstsammlungen,
Dresden; photo (from
facsimile edition published by
Edition Leipzig) Peter
Kibbles

VIII	VI	VII	XIII
LA JUSTICE	L'AMOUREUX.	LE CHARIOT	LA MORT

Top: Modern Swiss tarot cards. Collection Evelyn Goshawk; photo Peter Kibbles

Lower: Modern Sicilian tarot cards. Collection Evelyn Goshawk; photo Peter Kibbles

deterrent to the frequent presentation of this alluring hypothesis.

As we have already seen, ordinary cards as described by Johannes cannot have been introduced into Europe by the gypsies since they were known in Basle some forty years before the gypsies reached that city, where they are first recorded in 1414. On the other hand, while it is chronologically possible for the gypsies to have brought trumps with them, since both appeared at about that time, there are two considera-

46

tions which make it difficult to believe that they did so. In the first place there are no records of the use of the tarot in India, whence the gypsies originally came, or in the intervening countries, such as Afghanistan, Persia and Turkey, through which they passed. In the second place, in the fifteenth century the gypsies had no need to use a secret writing; they were recognized as religious pilgrims by popes and bishops and princes and municipalities and were treated as honoured guests. It was not until 1499, in which year Ferdinand and Isabella banished them from Spain, that oppression of the gypsies set in. In the sixteenth century the governments of Europe treated them with barbarity, vying with each other in banishing, outlawing and slaying them; but this was too late by far to have had any influence on the design or introduction of the tarot.

Turning to the motives behind the designing of the tarot, these are ascribed by the remote past school of thought either to a desire to explain, or an anxiety to preserve, certain religious mysteries. The first theory is that in Egyptian pre-history the figures were painted in niches in temple walls, eleven to the north and eleven to the south, and their meanings revealed, one by one, to the novices as they advanced in knowledge. The second suggests that a conclave of hierophants, foreseeing the collapse of their order, decided to preserve their esoteric doctrines by entrusting them to the everlasting strength of man's eternal weakness for gaming. Neither hypothesis is sustained by more than imagination.

The theory of a sectarian origin rests upon a tripod of needs; firstly for keeping in touch with a flock mainly illiterate, scattered through several countries and speaking a variety of languages; secondly for teaching aids internationally usable; and thirdly for mutual encouragement of the faithful in between the infrequent visits of the pastors. It is difficult to think of anything that better suits this range of requirements than a pack of cards. Moreover, this thesis does not stand alone. It is supported by Harold Bayley's argument that some heretics signalled to each other by means of water-marks, strengthened by H. Clea's positive statement of the existence of secret passwords and a subterranean network of unorthodox beliefs and re-inforced by Professor Gabrielle Rossetti's insistence, in his *Disquisition on the Anti-papal Spirit*, on the 'masked language of the secret anti-papal sects'.

In the nature of things the meanings here attached to the individual cards can only be guessed; but those guesses are reasoned guesses in accordance with the general beliefs of the times and with the creed of the Waldenses in particular. Both can easily be verified from the massive literature readily available in most European languages, whereas there is no such easy comparison for any interpretation claiming a basis in the darker secrets of the hermetic books.

We are then in a position to presume for the tarot an origin among the so-called heretics, or reformers, of the fifteenth century.

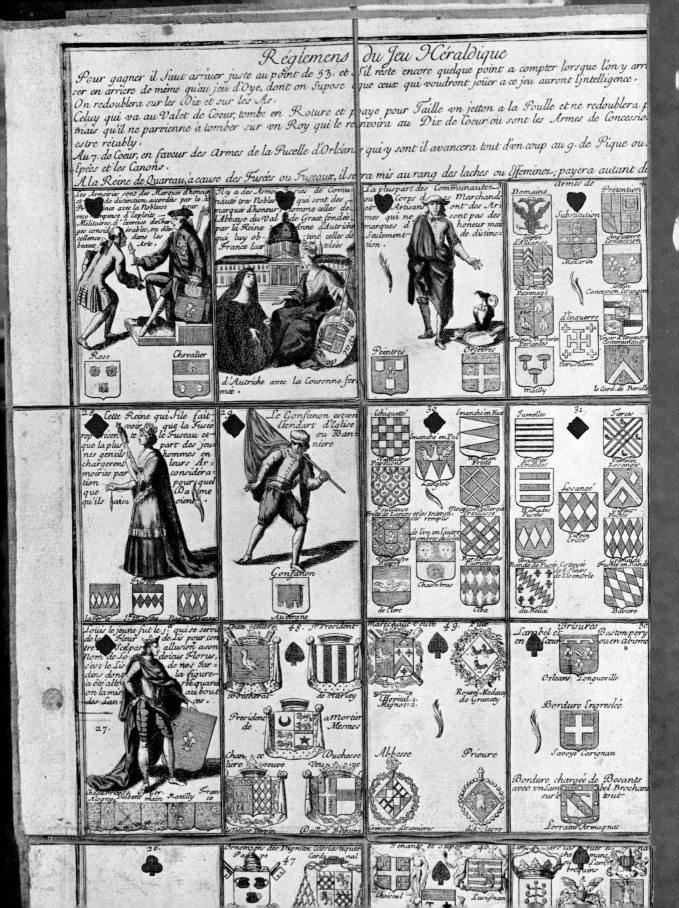

Réglemens du Jeu Héraldique

Pour gagner il faut arriver juste au point de 53. et s'il reste encore quelque point a compter lorsque l'on y arrive se mettre en arrière de même qu'au jeu d'Oye, dont on suppose que ceux qui voudront jouer a ce jeu auront l'intelligence.

On redoublera sur les Dix et sur les As.

Celuy qui va au Valet de Coeur, tombe en Roture et paye pour Taille un jetton a la Poulle et ne redoublera mais qu'il ne parvienne à tomber sur un Roy qui le renvoira au Dix de Coeur ou sont les Armes de Concession estre retably.

Au 7. de Coeur, en faveur des Armes de la Pucelle d'Orléans qui y sont il avancera tout d'un coup au 9. de Pique ou Epées et les Canons.

A la Reine de Quareau, à cause des Fusées ou Fuseaux, il sera mis au rang des laches ou Effeminez; payera autant de

Les Armoiries sont des Marques d'honneur et de distinction accordées par le Prince avec la Noblesse pour reconpense d'exploits Militaires, d'Exercice de Charges considerables, d'excellence dans les beaux Arts.

Rose — Chevalier

Il y a des Armoiries de Communauté très Nobles qui sont des marques d'honneur comme celles de l'Abbaye du Val de Grace, fondée par la Reine Anne d'Autriche qui luy obtint celles de France car elles sont escartelées.

d'Autriche avec la Couronne fermée.

La pluspart des Communautez ou Corps des Marchands et Artisans ont des Armes qui ne sont pas des marques d'honneur mais seulement de distinction.

Peintres — Orfevres

Armes de Domaine — Prétention — Imperiale d'Alliance — Substitution — Angleterre Concession — Due d'Yorc Patronage — Mazarin — Utin Concession Étrangere — Cardinal Barberin Parlantes — Voyer d'Argenson Communauté — d'Inguerre — Mailly — Ierusalem — le Card. de Berulle

28. Cette Reine qui file fait voir que la Fusée représente le Fuseau et que la pluspart des jeunes gentilshommes chargeront leurs Armoiries par considération pour quelque Dame qu'ils aimoient.

Fusée
la Ferté — St. Marthe — Nagu Varennes

29. Le Gonfanon estant l'étendart d'Eglise ou Bannière.

Gonfanon
Auvergne

30. Echiquette — Emanché en Face — Emanché en Pal — Vastadour Papillonne — Herman Frette — Langlois — Feuillure Frete de Lances et les Interstices remplis de l'un en l'autre et ombre de Soleil — Moivia Villeneuve d'Apru — Hillergie Treslisse — Barth Emanche Plumetté — Chardebras — de Clerc — Alba

31. Jumelles — Tierces — Gontier Amades — Pierelon Losanges — Hamades Fusées — Losangé — Clisson Fusele — Turpin Crissé — Bouillier Bande de Fusée — Cottayée de 6. fleurs de Lis en Orle — Fronfalé Fusele en Bande — du Bellai — Baviere

Loüis le jeune fut le 1.er qui se servit de la Fleur de Lis pour contre Scel par allusion a son Nom de Loüis ou doüis Florus, c'est le Lis de nos Jardins dont la figure a été alterée quand on la mis au bout des Lances.
27.
Chaudrier Alsony — Gilbert Germain — Ramilly Franc

48. Chancelier — 1.er Président — Mareschalle veuve — 49. Fille — Boucherat — de Harlay — l'Hospital. 1. Mignot. 2. — Rouxel Medau de Grancey — Lambel en Coeur — Brisures Baston peri en bande ou en abisme — Orleans — Longueville — Président de Mortier — Mesmes — Chancelière veuve — Duchesse veuve — Abbesse — Prieure — Bordure Engreslée — le Tellier Morpin — Daillon Bethune — Croyant d'inumieres — d'Alegre — Savoye Carignan — Bordure chargée de Besants avec un Lambel Brochant sur le tout — Lorraine Armagnac

26.
Ornemens des Dignitez Ecclesiastiques — Pape — 47 Cardinal — Tenants et Suports 46 — Choiseul — Lusignan

The second pack of which we have individual knowledge was painted in 1415 for Filippo Maria Visconti, Duke of Milan, a member of a family which had been of sovereign rank in northern Italy since the beginning of the thirteenth century.

The pack, which is said to have been painted by the Duke's secretary, Marzia de Tortona, has ninety-seven cards, made up of seventy-eight cards of the normal tarot pack with an additional nineteen trumps. These additions represent three theological virtues, Faith, Hope and Charity; the cardinal virtue of Prudence; the four elements of mediaeval philosophy, Fire, Water, Earth and Air; ten signs of the Zodiac, the Scales, the Virgin, the Scorpion, the Ram, the Goat, the Archer, the Crab, the Fishes, the Water-carrier and the Lion; and one other card, the Bull. The court cards and the trumps were unnamed and un-numbered, but in later packs of this type the trumps, with the exception of the last five, are numbered from 1 to 35. Two other features peculiar to this pack are the designer's curious view of knights—he has drawn those of cups and of coins as half monster and the other two as centaurs—and his manner of displaying the swords, which are straight and set out more clearly than the normal curved swords of Italian cards.

According to tradition this sequence, known as the Florentine *minchiate* pack, was invented by Michelangelo to help him teach arithmetic to the children of Florence. Alas for the tradition, Michelangelo was not born until another sixty years had elapsed; but there may well be some truth in the legend that these cards were used in some way as visual aids to teaching. With the additional trumps the cards seem to be the predecessors by, about, half a century of the so-called *Tarocchi of Mantegna*, and they certainly were educational.

See colour illustration page 44

The *Tarocchi of Mantegna*, which are neither *tarocchi* nor by Mantegna, and for that matter are not even playing cards, are a series of five sets of ten prints consisting of: the Ranks and Conditions of Men, from beggar to Pope; Apollo and the Nine Muses; the seven Liberal Arts to which have been added the three transcendental studies of Poetry, Philosophy and Theology; the seven Virtues, four cardinal and three theological, together with Chronico, the Genius of Time, Cosmico the Genius of the Universe, and Iliaco, the Genius of the Sun; and the seven Planets supplemented by the three Outer Spheres, comprising the Sphere of the Fixed Stars, the Primum Mobile or Outer Sphere, and the Empyrean or abode of Heavenly Wisdom, together forming the Ptolemaic order of the Universe which was unreservedly accepted until the middle of the fifteenth century. These prints appear to be, and are

Jeu Héraldique by Daumont, Paris 1698. From an uncut sheet of fifty-two cards. Bowes Museum, Durham

generally acknowledged as some sort of handbook or manual of the mediaeval idea of Creation, with all its various aspects carefully classified. Their purpose was clearly instructive, though they seem to be harking back to the Trivium and Quadrivium of the Middle Ages; but the Renaissance was as much the rebirth of things that had gone before and been lost as the birth of new ideas, new systems and new knowledge.

If the Florentine *minchiate* pack was designed primarily as an aid to education, the next type of pack of which we hear, known as the 'Bologna Tarots' or, more generally, *tarocchini*, was planned for a particular game. The sequence had no new designs but was achieved by omitting from the tarot pack the twos, threes, fours and fives of each suit, and rearranging the order of the trumps, of which only 5 to 16 are numbered. This gave a pack of sixty-two cards, which, obviously, was far less unwieldy than the *minchiate* pack. Traditionally the pack was devised by Francesco Fibbia, Prince of Pisa and Duke of Lucca, living in Bologna, in banishment, and the resulting game was said to have been so pleasing to the court that the Prince was rewarded with the privilege of displaying his arms on the queen of batons and those of his wife on the queen of coins. This story was challenged by the same Robert Steele whose lecture of 31 May 1900 has already been quoted. He said that he could find no evidence that cards with these particular armorial devices had ever been printed. One further interesting fact about this pack is that early in the eighteenth century the Empress and the Emperor and the Popess and the Pope were replaced by four Moors, a change due, in all probability, to political circumstances. In 1513 the independent Republic of Bologna acknowledged the sovereignty of the Pope (Julius II) and it may well be that some two hundred years later his successor used his authority to rectify some suspected affront to the papacy.

One further very early pack is worth mentioning since at least forty-eight of the cards are still in existence, no less than thirty-five of them in the Pierpont Morgan Library in New York. These remains of a tarot pack—all the trumps survive—have been exhaustively investigated by Gertrude Oakley, who shows that they were painted by Bonifacio Bembo for the Visconti-Sforza family in, or very soon after, the year 1450. It is most interesting to find that Mrs Oakley remarks that 'The Cards are painted and illuminated on heavy cardboard. Each card measures 175 × 87 millimetres, and is very thick, so thick that it is hard to imagine the set having been used for actual play'.

To whatever uses princes and pastors may have put the trumps of the tarot, the princes, at least, used the rest of the pack, that is to say the numbered and court cards, for playing games and gambling. We cannot be certain of the games played, but if yet another legend is to be believed, *trappola* is the oldest game of all. Three other games of very early date were Hazard, said to have been played by Filippo

Maria Visconti, and Bassett and Flush, both mentioned by Lorenzo the Magnificent in a *canzone* written when he was a young man, probably about 1470. Bassett is also mentioned in the sermon quoted by Robert Steele. In his lines Lorenzo says, 'This Bassett is a very quick game. . . . The only trouble is that it does not last long'; and he goes on to say that *Il Frusso*, otherwise *Primero* or Flush, 'is a cursed game. But nowadays even the peasants play it.'

The lives of princes and their courtiers are ruled by protocol; but games know no such artificial boundaries. Like manners and customs and fashions they descend from the higher levels of society to the lower, the latter copying and adopting the habits of the former. What yesterday was the pastime of princes today becomes the game of the people. So it was with playing cards, with ordinary men and women soon becoming desirous of experiencing the pleasures and excitements of the card table. Their favourite game was *trappola* which required a thirty-six-card pack consisting of ace, two, seven, eight, nine, ten, knave, knight and king, in each of the four suits of cups, swords, coins and batons. The designs were no different from those of the tarot packs. A game for gambling, and like gambling 'a gentle witchery', *trappola* proved immensely popular and quickly emigrated to foreign countries.

See colour illustration page 124

5

The spread of the new influence

The love of card games proved highly contagious, in the manner of a pandemic disease infecting people far and wide. Something had to be done and since this offered to men of enterprise an opportunity of making money something was done quickly. Master card makers set up their own workshops and began quantity production. This was made possible by the use of stencils and by reducing the pack to fifty-two cards, which was achieved by dropping all the trumps and leaving out the knaves. Even if the general run of people had been able to afford hand-painted cards it would have been impossible to produce them in anything approaching the required numbers. Sometimes both the outlines of the designs and the colours were stencilled, in which case as many stencils as there were colours were required. Sometimes only the outlines were stencilled and the colours applied by hand, which may have taken longer but which generally achieved a better result. Correct registration, or positioning, of successive stencils was not easy, for if the stencils were not accurately registered the colours overlapped their allotted space.

The demand for cards increased despite the strenuous opposition of the Church. Certainly the sermons of St Bernardino of Siena, he of the sharp features, pointed chin, emaciated frame and squalid attire, resulted in bonfires of playing cards and throngs of penitent gamblers. But the gamblers appear to have returned quickly to their former play, since little impression in the long run was made on card playing, which continued as feverishly as ever. But if card playing was not diminished, if the number of gamblers was no less, there was at least a reduction in the price of cards. In 1454 the sum paid for a pack for the Dauphin of France was 5 sous tournois, which was just about one thousandth of the amount paid thirty-nine years earlier for the Duke of Milan's pack.

We cannot be certain of the exact geographical sequence followed by cards. Presumably they first spread throughout Italy, where in the course of time a dozen or so packs, each with variations of the original design came into being. If the chronology of extant records is adhered to, we then turn to Regensburg, or Ratisbon, where cards were prohibited in 1378, and secondly to Belgium: for there are two entries for *speelquarten* in the 1379 accounts of the Dukedom of Brabant, one for the 13th of May and one for the 28th of June. But change of country without change of design need not greatly concern us, and there is nothing to suggest that the citizens of Regensburg or the Duke and Duchess of Brabant played with cards of any design other than Italian. Nor do we know what games they played. For the first modification, one of arrangement as much as of design, we must turn to Spain, noting, *en passant,* that M. d'Allemagne, the great French authority, has suggested that cards reached Spain in Flemish bottoms out of Rouen.

By whatever route they travelled, the cards favoured by the Spaniards had the Italian suit marks—cups, swords, coins and batons. No trumps made their way into the Peninsular, even in the more expensive packs. At first glance this seems peculiar since the tarot was popular in neighbouring Southern France, understandably so when it is recalled that the western valleys of the Cottian Alps, where the heretics had taken refuge, run down into the province of Dauphiné. At second glance, however, the reason is apparent. In 1194 Alphonso II of Aragon issued a decree:

> Wherefore, in imitation of our predecessors, and in due
> obedience to the canons; since they judged that heretics, who
> are cast out from the sight of God and all Catholics, ought
> everywhere to be condemned and persecuted: therefore, as
> enemies of Christ and the Christian Religion, and as public
> foes both of ourself and of our Kingdom, we command forthwith
> to depart and banish themselves those who are called Valdenses
> or Insabbatati or Poor Men of Lyons, and all other heretics
> without number who have been anathematised by the Holy
> Church; so that they should evacuate the whole of our
> Kingdom and Lordship.

The Aragonese persecuted the heretics with particular severity. By nature strongly conservative, the Aragonese, urged on by Church and State, did not rest in their oppression of the heretics until the latter had vanished completely from those parts. The outcome of this persecution was 'No heretics, no Tarot'.

Cards having arrived, and the Italian suit marks accepted, the Spaniards made a number of changes in the designs, the alterations consisting, in the main, of an exact reversal of some of the original details, as if to show Spanish freedom from Italian influence. The Spanish kings, for instance, all stand instead of being seated; the curved and slim Italian rapiers becoming straight, heavy, two-edged Roman swords; the narrow batons are turned into great cudgels such as Hercules is apt to carry in drawings illustrating his labours, and often have knobs or leaves on the side; and both kinds of weapon are set out straight, separate and generally parallel to one another instead of being bunched together or interlaced. That this weapon arrangement, which enables a player to see at a glance the exact number of swords or batons is an immense improvement on the original was perhaps the happy outcome of a show of independence. Perhaps it was brought about by the love of gambling shown by the Spanish; for to the inveterate gambler clarity is all important.

53

Spanish cards, stencilled, by
J. Fouquet, c. 1780–90.
Collection Hans Janssen

The few innovations that were made included the embellishment of the centre coin of the five of coins with the heads of a king and queen, generally thought to be Ferdinand and Isabella, the energetic couple who united Spain. The queens are replaced by mounted knights. The ace of coins generally displays the arms of Spain, and the ace of swords has a sword belt held up by a small boy. The cards, which are smaller than the Italian, were given bright colours—oranges and greens, yellows, blues and reds. The names of the suits when translated into Spanish were *caliz* (later *copas*), *espadas*, *cros* and *bastos*; and the courts were called *rey*, *caballo* or *caballero* and *sota*.

That these modifications of the original Italian design took place soon after the introduction of cards into Spain is, strictly speaking, conjectural: for no cards earlier than the last quarter of the sixteenth century have come to light. That there are no survivors of the first century or century and a half of Spanish cards seems strange, due, perhaps, to the perpetual eagerness of all ranks of Spanish society for card playing, which kept every pack in constant use until it was worn out. It is also curious that the majority of cards for the Spanish market appear to have been manufactured in France. In all probability the largest shipments were from Toulouse and Thiers; but the card masters of Limoges also did a steady trade with Spain, as did their competitors in Rouen, who also supplied the Portuguese market.

The National game which claimed so much of Spaniards' devoted

54

attention was *hombre*, or 'the man', played with a pack of forty cards, the eight, nine and ten of each suit being discarded. Originally intended for two players, the game was adapted by the Spaniards for three, a change which brought about the introduction of triangular card tables specially made for the purpose. *Ombre*, as the name became in English, is described by Alexander Pope in 'The Rape of the Lock', written in 1714 to appease Miss Belle Fermor whom Lord Petre had offended by cutting off a lock of her hair.

Another, earlier game played by the Spaniards was *renegado*, also for three players, which may have been an adaptation of the Italian game of *ronfa*, mentioned along with *basset* in the sermon produced by Mr Steele. And a third was *la luette*, a fifteenth-century game known to Rabelais's Gargantua, and later often called *alluette*. Originally played in northern Spain, it became popular along the west coast of France, attracting players ever further north until it reached Brittany, where it came to rest. After a while interest declined and it is now a long time since the game was played by other than Bretons. Because of this restriction to the one area the pack is sometimes described erroneously as a French regional design.

In the early packs of this game, the centre coin of the 5 of coins had the heads of a man and woman facing each other, a drawing so reminiscent of Ferdinand and Isabella in other packs that it seems safe to place the origins of this pack in the fifteenth century. Some two hundred years ago the picture was replaced by one of a young man about to kiss a bare-breasted young woman, from which the card, already named Robino, acquired the additional title of The Indecorous. The ace of cups one might think equally deserving of the epithet. A bare-bosomed woman, seen only in profile, juts out from each side of the cup to form a handle, looking rather like a ship's figurehead.

The most interesting characteristic of this pack is the replacement of the *caballero*, or knight, by a mounted woman, unarmed and riding astride. Considering that the Spaniards were at pains to replace the queen in the Italian sequence with a *caballero*, this, the sole example of a woman in a Spanish pack, is most surprising. Can she have been introduced as a compliment to Annoof Brittany, a veritable Breton of Bretons?

Other features of this pack include a cow lying beneath the suit signs of the two of cups, the card being called *la vache*; and a child swinging on a rope suspended from the boughs of the two of batons with a dog bounding from the foot of one.

The pip cards of the suit of batons are decorated with arrows instead of the fleur-de-lis found in the original design. The centre coin of the 3 of that suit has the head and shoulders of a man wearing epaulets, known as *Monsieur*. The 3 of cups has the bust of a woman above the central cup, known as *Madame*. The 9 of cups is known as *le grand neuf* and the 9 of coins as *le petit neuf*.

Card history in Portugal appears to have followed a similar pattern

Opposite and above: Court cards from a pack by Pierre Maréchal, Rouen 1567. Photo by *County Life*

to that of Spain. The Portuguese, too, adopted the re-drawn Italian suit marks, and they, too, imported most of their cards from France. From both countries, in each of which the Renaissance was largely characterized by exploration and colonization, cards of the same type flowed overseas. Under the inspiration and guidance first of Henry the Navigator (1394–1460) and then of John II and Manoel I, the Portuguese mariners charted thousands of miles of the west African coast, including the Congo river; they discovered the Azores, rounded the Cape of Storms, re-named the Cape of Good Hope by the king in the confident expectation of finding a new route to India, reached Brazil and established themselves in Goa, Ceylon and Malacca. Christopher Columbus, a Genoese under the patronage of Isabella of Spain, discovered America; Cortez conquered Mexico and the Aztecs and lined Spanish coffers with gold and silver; Magellan, a Portuguese in the service of Spain, discovered the straits named after him when on a voyage round the world which ended in the Philippines; and Pizarro conquered Peru and the Incas and sent yet more gold back to the motherland. And wherever these hardy sailors and their accompanying soldiers travelled they took with them their passion for gambling and card playing. Montezuma himself is said to have taken pleasure in watching Spanish soldiers play at 'Cardes and Dyce'. No doubt the Sultan of Malacca and the Samuri of Calicut derived equal gratification from watching the card playing of the men commanded by Alfonso d'Albuquerque, 'The Portuguese Mars'. But watching, like patriotism, was not enough. The inhabitants joined in, and in a short time, apparently, were making their own cards. Having no paper they drew their designs on skin or bark, drawing and painting in their own native style. While the final results sometimes seem crude and the figures childlike, the original Spanish/Portuguese inspiration is easily discernible. One of the most interesting series of such cards is in the South West Museum of California. Hand-painted on skin by Apache Indians, at times immature and coarsely executed, the packs show faithfulness to the Spanish originals although they all date from the second half of the nineteenth century.

Germany and the great leap forward

6

Playing cards had three main offshoots. The first, as we have seen, travelled northwestward and westward into Belgium, France, Spain and Portugal; the second went northward through Switzerland into southwest Germany; while the third journeyed northeastward into Austria, Bohemia, Silesia and as far as Poland. Of these Spain was the first to modify the original design, and Germany the first to introduce an entirely new pack. The introduction was not effected immediately.

In her early years as a card playing country, Germany used the Italian pack for the game of *lansquenet*, a simple game of mere chance and a variation of *bassett*, which in its turn was, presumably, imported from Italy together with the first cards. Germans were no more impervious to the fascination of card games than anybody else, and in the early fourteenth and fifteenth centuries became as excited by them as were later generations by the legend of the Lorelei. As a result, they gambled so persistently and with such fervour that many cities found it necessary to place cards under an interdiction. Prohibitions were enforced in Ulm in 1397, in Augsburg in 1400 and 1403, and 1406 elsewhere.

Where the Spaniards demonstrated their independence of Italian influence while acknowledging their affinity with another Latin race, the Germans showed their complete freedom of taste in these matters. Not for them to follow slavishly in the footsteps of the artists of Cremona, Ferrara and Mantua and tamely accept swords and cups, coins and clubs. As a start they introduced bells (*schellen*) and hearts (*herzen*), leaves (*grün* or *laub*) and acorns (*eicheln*) as suit signs, and these became the national sequence. The divisions of society have been seen in these suit marks just as they were in the Italian symbols. Bells, that is hawk-bells, are said to stand for the nobility because of their love of falconry; hearts for the Church; leaves for the middle classes; and acorns for the peasants.

Next, the German card masters discarded the ace, leaving the 2, or *daus*, as the highest card, and making a pack of forty-eight. Why this was so is not known, for no game for that number of cards has yet come to light. Then, for a hundred years or so, the 10 was represented by a flag flying in the breeze with a Roman X at the head of the card. Yet a fourth variation in the early packs lay in the numerical cards of the suits of hearts and bells being painted red, of leaves and acorns green, and all the court cards red and green. The Germans copied the Spaniards in one thing only. They would not accept the queen,

Three *obers*, German woodcut,
c. 1640.
Slide collection Roger Tilley

the court cards being *könig*, *obermann* and *untermann*, the last two being
known as *ober* and *unter* for short.

The first German cards, like the Italian, were hand-painted or
stencilled, and some of the former were lovely works of art specially
commissioned by princes and plutocrats as much for status symbols
as for play. The painted Stuttgart cards, dated 1437, with suits of
ducks and falcons, stags and dogs, and vignettes of the chase were
probably of this nature; and the Ambras Princely Hunting Cards of
about 1450 were in much the same mould.

Big changes in the method of production were soon on the way.
Travelling hard on the heels of playing cards, Italians carried the art
and mystery of paper making into Germany, where the first mill,
established at Nuremburg, went into production in 1390. Paper was
made from discarded rags of all kinds, including cast-off garments
and, if we are to believe the wandering Arabian physician Abdol-
latiph, even the cloth used to enwrap Egyptian mummies. In 1373,
Venice, in order to safeguard her paper production, strictly prohibited
the export of all kinds of rags, and the historian Simeon Luce (as
quoted by the learned M. Henri Bouchot) points out that 'The fourteenth century by the fact alone that it is the century of body linen
is the indispensible preparer of Printing.' As soon as paper was produced in quantity and became cheaper than parchment the engravers

in the persons of the goldsmiths, enamellists and monumental brass designers seized upon the new material and the art of wood-engraving, as known in the west, was born.

Little time was lost by the German card masters in adapting the new process to the needs of their businesses, and soon quantities of cards were leaving their workshops. An original manuscript, completed in 1474, chronicling the history of the city of Ulm, records that 'Playing cards were sent in large bales into Italy, Sicily and other places by sea, getting in exchange spices and other merchandise.' And the other side of the picture is shown by a decree of the Signoria of Venice, of which the following is a translation of part:

> MCCCCXLI. October 11th. Whereas the art and mystery of making playing cards and printed figures, which is used at Venice, has fallen to total decay: and this in consequence of the great quantity of playing cards and coloured figures printed, which are made out of Venice; let it be ordered and established that, from this time in future, no work of the said art, that is printed on cloth, or paper, that is to say altar pieces (or images) and playing cards, shall be allowed to be brought or imported into this city, under pain of forfeiting the work so imported, and xxx livres and xxII soldi.

Before the half century was out engraving on copper began to take the place of woodcutting, though the latter remained the medium for mass-production. During the second half of the fifteenth century and the beginning of the sixteenth some of the finest engravers the world has ever known practised their art, and their playing cards reached a standard seldom equalled and never surpassed. These Germans let their imaginations run riot. Never content to engrave cards with nothing more than the simple number of suit signs, they decorated the faces with pictures of men and women, animals and birds. Nor did that satisfy these men of genius. Within the four corners of their copper plates were miniatures of infinite charm based on non-standard suit signs of every sort and kind—pinks, roses and columbines, unicorns and rabbits and apes, books and vases, helmets and escutcheons and many another strange device.

Of the succession of inspired engravers who devoted some of their brilliant talent to playing cards, the first was the Master of the Playing Cards (*der Meister der Spielkarten*). Since his style is reflected in the work of the unknown artist responsible for the engraving generally accepted by art historians as the earliest known, a Flagellation of Christ bearing the date 1446, the Master of the Playing Cards must have been born early in the century. He is the first known copper engraver; his work included forty-four known engravings in addition to sixty-six playing cards; the latter were not incised until 1453–54.

Next in succession comes the Master of the Monogram ES, some-

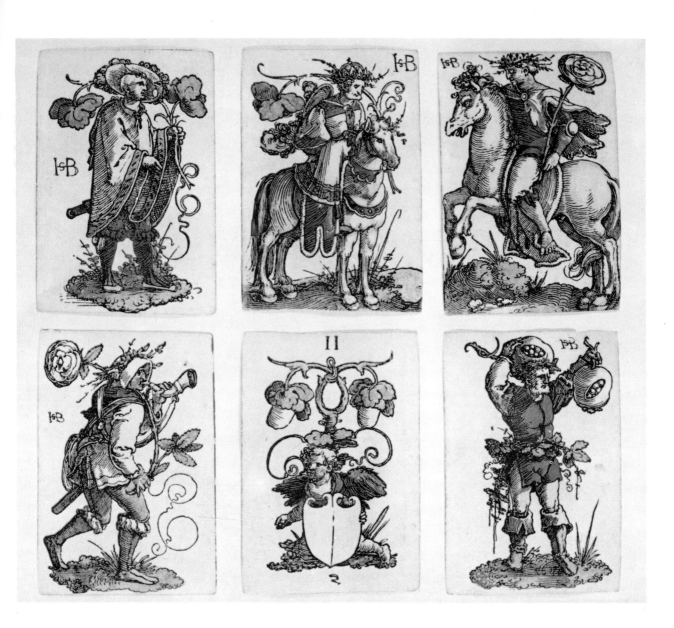

Cards from a sixteenth-
century German pack. Suits
are roses, pomegranates, vine
leaves and acorns. The kings
are mounted; *obers* and *unters*
are depicted as peasants.
ISP or ISB is inscribed on some
of the cards.
Bodleian Library, Oxford

times known as the Master of the year 1466 from a date on one of his
plates, who was responsible for two packs of cards. Though his style
owes much to the Master of the Playing Cards, he did not attain high
standing as an artist, mainly because of his failure to master perspective.
He was, however, technically brilliant, and it was as a technician of
engraving that he had a considerable effect upon Martin Schöngauer
(*c.* 1445–99), an artist of high calibre whom the French authority
the Vicomte Delaborde classes with Dürer and Holbein. Designs by
Martin Schöngauer were used, even if he did not engrave them him-

60

self, in a pack which is partly attributed to Israhel von Meckensen, an artist much influenced by his 'partner of the pack' though he did not reach his standard.

Other, though not necessarily connected, artists were the Master of the Monogram PW, who about the year 1500 engraved some small round cards; Hans Sebald Beham (1500–50), whose surviving work includes a sheet of playing cards; Edward Schön, whose earliest work is dated 1515 and his last 1542, who engraved some round cards with five suits, hares, rabbits, pinks, roses and columbines; Virgil Solis (1514–62), a prolific illustrator best known for his two editions of the Bible, whose playing cards with suits of lions, monkeys, peacocks and parrots are superb even if his general work was low in quality, and Jost Ammon (1539–91), whose output of engravings for miscellaneous purposes, such as title pages for books, was immense, and who cut the woodcuts for a beautiful pack of cards published as a small book under the title of *The Book of Trades*, with suits of winepots, printers' See colour illustration page 45 pads, drinking cups and books. Each card carries some improving lines, in Latin at the head and in High German at the foot. For example, the 3 of printers' pads shows an elegantly dressed couple sitting at a table beneath three pads, a lighted candle on the table, the man seated on a wooden stool with cards in his right hand and the lady sitting opposite him in a woven cane chair with cards in her left hand, a goblet in her right and a dog at her feet. Beneath is the verse:

Du hast gewonnen edler Hort,
Ich will nun dein sein hic und dort,
Da lebet Gott, wo Mann und Weib
Zwen Menschen sein, ein Seel, ein Leib.

[You have won, noble Protector,
I will now be yours for ever,
There lives God, where man and wife
Two beings are, one soul, one body.]

Jost Ammon may have obtained the idea for this pack from Rodericus Zamorensis' *Spiegel des menslichen Lebens* published by Gunther Zainer in 1477. Of it Sir Sydney Cockerell writes: 'One may say that the book itself, one of the most popular of the Middle Ages, runs through all the conditions and occupations of men as then existing, from the Pope and Kaiser down to the field labourer.'

From about 1550 to 1650 there was a general decline in the standard of engraving, a decline coincident with a vast increase in the production of engravings due to the huge demand for holy pictures, block books, indulgences and so forth. One exception to this general rule was a pack of thirty-six cards printed from silver plates in the second half of the seventeenth century. Examples are to be found in the collection of the United States Playing Card Company, and six of them were

used by Catherine Perry Hargrave as illustrations in her book *A History of Playing Cards*. They are charming, with delightful figures of little people and animals under, or beside, their suit sign. The engraving is generally attributed to the noted German engraver and goldsmith Georg Heinrich Bleich; but it is noteworthy that the *Thieme und Becker Allgemeines Lexikon der Bildenden Künstler*, a standard work, remarks: 'Mit dem Kartenspiel im Besitze des Grafen Fr von Rothernburg hat Bleich nichts zu tun.'

Replicas of the enchanting designs on the cards of the Master of the Playing Cards have been traced by German and American scholars in several Bibles and prayer-books. Judging by the postures of some of the figures, in particular a small bear which on one of the cards appears to be climbing non-existing scroll-work, the miniatures came before the cards. It is not possible to prove that one was copied from the other, or, alternatively, that both were copied from the same model book, though the latter is believed to be the case. In his fascinating and beautifully produced book, *Gutenberg and the Master of the Playing Cards*, Dr Hellmut Lehmann-Haupt points out that the Master and Gutenberg were 'actively working in related fields in Mainz in the early 1450s . . . and it is inconceivable that they should not have known one another' And he argues convincingly that Gutenberg's dream was not limited to the creation of a machine that would reproduce only the written word but extended to the reproduction of coloured initials, scroll-work and miniatures. To achieve this he must either have engraved the necessary copper plates himself or hired someone to do so for him; and Dr Lehmann-Haupt believes that the

Cards from a sixteenth-century German woodcut pack, thought to be by Jost Ammon. Suits are parakeets, roses, acorns and bells. Female figures appear in place of the *obers*.
Bodleian Library, Oxford

Cards from a North-west German pack, engraved and hand-coloured, *c.* 1870. Scenic aces.
Collection Evelyn Goshawk; photo Peter Kibbles

Master of the Playing Cards was engaged for, and upon, this work. Later, Gutenberg must have realized that he could not pursue these experiments further. *Nolens volens* he released the plates. His copper engraver—in other words the Master of the Playing Cards—looked for an opportunity to employ his printing material in an economically productive way. He decided to use the already existing intaglio plates to print a set of playing cards; he supplemented his material by adding cards which required large figures, and other cards which were to be printed not from the composite plates with individually mounted little figures but from newly engraved whole plates.

Finally Dr Lehmann-Haupt quotes Dr Rosenfeld of Munich as writing in a review of an article by Lehmann-Haupt (in *Papers of the Biographical Society of America* Vol. 58) that preceded the book:

> The Master of the Playing Cards is no longer to be considered an ingenious inventor, but a skilful copper engraver following available models. His playing cards, to be sure, have been imitated by other artists, since the patrons of the fine arts enjoyed these bizarre, but impracticable, cards and saved them from oblivion by pasting them into books and manuscripts. For the history of playing cards, these particular cards have become, unfortunately, a blind alley.

It may well be that the work of the Master of the Playing Cards is a blind alley so far as the history of playing cards is concerned. On the other hand, the inventions of the printing press and copper engraving, with both of which he was so intimately concerned, were powerful influences in the development of the Renaissance of northern Europe.

With the arrival of the northern Renaissance fundamental and far-reaching changes took place. Printing reduced the need for memorization. Erasmus, who became the greatest scholar of the day, the intellectual dictator of the age and the most significant figure in the northern Renaissance, recommended in his *Liberal Education of Boys from the Beginning* that children should be taught reading, writing and drawing at their mother's knee and be spared the usual floggings, and the teachers of the period began to encourage their pupils with offers of prizes and with praise of the pleasures of scholarship. Montaigne's father first taught him Greek by writing letters and words on the backs of cards and then inventing a game to be played with them. In this freer atmosphere one of the most famous packs of cards was invented, and with it was founded a tradition which developed and flourished over the succeeding centuries.

The inventor was Thomas Murner, a noted German satirist and a Franciscan monk, who had led the roving life of a scholar and poet through Germany and Switzerland. In 1507, while lecturing in philosophy at the University of Cracow, he designed a pack which harked back to one of the earliest purposes of playing cards—that of teaching. Intended to help his students in the study of logic, the pack was published in book form. The pack had ten logical cards and pip cards with sixteen suit signs—the old German signs of bells, hearts and acorns to which were added suns, moons, stars, shields, crowns, fish, lobsters, scorpions, grasshoppers, cats, caps, birds and serpents. The associated game was difficult to play and the information offered by the cards somewhat obscure; but the pupils acquitted themselves so well that their professor had some difficulty in clearing himself of a charge of witchcraft. A second edition of the cards was produced in Strasbourg in 1509.

A second pack of cards designed by Dr Murner, also printed at Strasbourg, was published in 1518. The game was much the same as the earlier one; but, the Institutes of Justinian requiring greater exposition than logic, the pack consisted of 120 cards, made up of twelve suits of ten cards each: The suit signs included buckets, beads, bells and bellows.

The Reformation, which Dr Murner was vigorously to oppose, was about to sweep across Europe. The famous ninety-five theses had already been nailed to the door of the church at Wittenberg. The movement brought with it a new and momentous phase in the history of education, which not only affected the whole school system but laid emphasis on the new methods of teaching. But before we can look at the reflections of the latter in the history of playing cards we must turn to developments in France.

7

Development of the French pack

An ordinance issued by the police of Lille, an ancient walled city and strong fortress on the frontier of Belgium, is the first unchallenged record of cards in France. Issued in 1382, it reads:

> De non juer as dez, as taules (au jeu de dames), as quartes, ni a nul aultre gieu. Que nuls ne soit si hardis uns ne aultres quelz que il soit qui depuis maintenant en avant en ceste ville, jucches, de jour ne de nuict, as dez, as taules, as quartes, ne a nul autre jeu quelconques.
> [Not to play dice, nor draughts (the game of ladies), nor card games, nor any kind of games. Let no-one be bold enough, whoever it might be, from this day onwards, in this town, to dare play, by day or by night, with dice, draughts, or any kind of game whatsoever.]

Card playing was forbidden because of the unfortunate effect it was thought to have on the standard of archery. Lolling around the card table, sometimes all night, not only came between the bowman and his bow but also clouded the eye and allowed the muscles to get flabby. In the event this proved to be a case of 'all talk and no cider', for the armies of Charles VI were roundly defeated by the English at Agincourt (1415) and elsewhere.

We do not know what game, or games, so bewitched the people of Lille that the police felt obliged to take action. But as the tarot was confined to the south of France, and as *piquet*, which became the national game, is probably a development of *ronfa*, it is reasonable to suppose that outside Provence and Dauphiné French players cut their card teeth on the latter. It is no more surprising that France and Spain should each derive their national game from the same model than that each country should get its idea of card games from a common source. *Basset*, or *bassette*, one of the other Italian games contemporary with *ronfa*, did not reach France until considerably later. Indeed, it is said to have been introduced into court circles by the Venetian ambassador, Justiniani, in the second half of the seventeenth century.

If there is nothing to wonder at in France starting her card playing career with an Italian game, it is, in the circumstances, odd, that when designing her own suit signs she should have based them on the German sequence. *Coeur* (heart) and *pique* (spade) are plainly copied from the German heart and leaf, the latter now turned upright instead of lying on its side, and *trèfle* (club) seems to be an adaptation of the acorn.

Only *carreau* (diamond), a paving stone of the encaustic, or wax-painted, kind used from the twelfth to the fifteenth century in church pavements, was an original idea. The Schoolmen, however, were consistent in seeing the divisions of society mirrored in these emblems. Hearts they claimed, stand for the Church; spades, spearheads, being the weapons of knights, for the aristocracy; diamonds, symbolizing that part of the church where the well-to-do were buried in the chancel, and clover, being the food of swine, for the peasantry.

No exact date can be given for the invention of the new signs; though if legend be correct in crediting them to Etienne de Vignoles, better known as La Hire, Knight and Hero, who died in 1442, then it must have been round 1430. La Hire is also supposed to have invented the French national game of *piquet*; and since the queen now appeared in the French pack, supplanting the *obermann*, he may have been responsible for her too. He was, after all, a staunch supporter of Joan of Arc. A tradition that *piquet* was inspired by a ballet, alternatively that La Hire was a balletomane, is improbably founded.

Having evolved the new, very easily stencilled suit signs, it was not long before the French card masters realized that it was quite unnecessary to engrave each court card separately as was the habit and

Below and over page
From a set of eighteenth-century French tarot cards. 'They fit into a beautiful gilt tooled, leather-bound box, made in imitation of a book, one side acting as a lid. Each side of the simulated book is tooled with the Royal Arms of France from which depends the chain and insignia of the Order of the Golden Fleece. Each coat of arms is surmounted by a Royal crown. At some time the shields of arms have been defaced, perhaps at the time of the 1791 Revolution when anti-Bourbon feeling was at its height.' The pack consists of twelve signs of the zodiac, four elements, twenty-two major trumps. The four suits represent Europe, Asia, Africa and America.
Bowes Museum, Durham

67

The four suits of the tarot pack
described on page 67

tradition of their German competitors. All that was required was
one wood block, or copper plate, with a king engraved on it, another
with a queen and a third with a knave, and all twelve court cards
could be printed from those three blocks alone if the suit signs were
later added by stencil. In consequence, while the German spent endless
care, separately designing and separately engraving each card in
every pack, the Frenchman completed, packed and despatched a
gross of packs before their competitors had turned out a dozen. German
markets were at the Frenchmen's mercy, and as the years passed by the
French sequence spread throughout the world.

At much the same time as they initiated the new symbols, the French
card masters adopted the national habit of naming their court cards.
No explanation of the choice of names has yet been discovered, and
as the names of kings and queens were seemingly dependent upon the
whim of the individual card master it is quite possible that there was
no reason behind the selection. Inexplicably, the names of the knaves

68

appear to have remained unchanged.

Early in their history the kings were Solomon, Augustus, Clovis and Constantine, while the queens were Elizabeth, Dido, Clothilde and Pantilsea; but towards the end of the reign of Henry IV, better known as Henry of Navarre (1553–1610), they settled down (except for short-term appearances of contemporary celebrities) as Charlemagne (hearts), David (spades), Caesar (diamonds) and Alexander (clubs), with Judith or Judic (hearts), Pallas (spades), Rachel (diamonds) and Argine (clubs) as the queens. Of these, only the queens invite much speculation, since the kings are clearly four of the great monarchs of early times, and the knaves, La Hire (hearts), Ogier, or Hogier (spades), Hector (diamonds) and Lancelot (clubs) are widely known. We have already mentioned La Hire. Ogier the Dane figures prominently in the *Chansons de Geste* as one of Charlemagne's knights. In a later romance he is carried off by the king's sister Morgan la Fay, who was a witch, as Merlin was the wizard, in the Arthurian legend.

Four of the twenty-two trump
cards from the pack described
on page 67, depicting Hearing,
Strength, Prudence and The
Sun.

The last two, it need scarcely be added, were famous as the hero of
Troy and as a knight of the Round Table respectively.

Père Daniel (1649–1728), in his *Dissertation sur l'origine du jeu de
piquet,* suggests that Judith was the Empress Judith who was the wife
of Louis le Debonnaire, son of Charlemagne, who died in AD 82.
Pallas, he considers, represents Joan of Arc; Rachel, he believes,
personifies Agnes Sorel, the beautiful mistress of Charles VII who

70

died in 1450; and Argine, an anagram of Regina, Mary of Aragon, wife to Charles VII. But as Père Daniel, a Jesuit historian, is said to have been not only without elegance but lacking an interest in the truth, we may, perhaps, disregard his views. Among other suggestions we find Judith standing for Isobel of Bavaria, wife of Charles VI and mother of Charles VII; Pallas for the Greek goddess of war; Rachel for Jacob's wife; and Argine for Juno, Queen of heaven. Père Menestrier (1631–1705), a Jesuit antiquarian, thought that the four queens were chosen because they represent four ways of ruling, that is by beauty, by wisdom, by piety and by right of birth. It is with a smile that one notes that Agnes Sorel, the courtesan, was a model for Mary, the Blessed Virgin, in a painting by Jean Fouquet, for a diptych for the Church of Nôtre Dame de Melun.

Element Terre.

Fifteenth-century French cards, few of which survive, vary much in quality. They all have considerable charm even when rather crudely drawn. Among sixteen made towards the end of the century and now in the collection of the United States Playing Card Company, the kings wear crowns a size or two too large for them, while the queens wear theirs on the backs of their heads, projecting not quite horizont-ally, with a kerchief thrown over them. All are 'richly and warmly wrapped' as the poet Skelton (1460–1529) says of the bishops of his time, in ample robes trimmed with ermine richly powdered with fleur-de-lis, an emblem which also appears at the tops of the kings' sceptres. In other court cards of the same period the kings and knaves have two-toned stockings, sometimes with ornate garters complete with tassel, and particoloured tunics and sleeves. One knave has a flower between his feet, and another a snail. The knaves are generally armed with a halberd, on which they lean, sometimes with a sword and dagger and at least one with a tremendous flail. On the other hand, four knaves, which Catherine Perry Hargrave, past Curator of the United States Playing Card Company collection, has dated circa 1440 which she says are the earliest printed playing cards of Europe that have ever been found, are not only better drawn, with more accurate stencilling, but have stronger colouring. They, too, are armed with halberds; spades, diamonds and clubs are accompanied by their dogs, and diamonds also has a rabbit popping out of its burrow between his feet. (Seguin and Gurney Benham date this pack c. 1490).

Element le Feu.

Earth and fire, two of the four elements from the pack on page 67

We may note that according to the Rev E. S. Taylor there was in existence towards the end of Henry II's reign (about 1550) a 'pack embroidered on white silk, enriched with silver . . . a chef d'oeuvre of art', and under Louis XIV they had 'cards engraved on mother of pearl'.

Duke of
Lennox Scott Dutches
of Buccleuh

Hamilton
Duke of Hamilton

Till now we have, in reality, followed the travels of card games: for the great mass of people was interested in games and gaming rather than elegant miniatures or expensive status symbols. It was *ronfa* and *basset* that emigrated from Italy to Germany, Belgium, France and Spain and Portugal with their overseas empires, and became nationalized as *landsknecht*, *piquet* and *ombre*, rather than swords and coins going forth and changing into spades and diamonds. With the end of the sixteenth century, however, the pack acquired a dual personality. Harking back to its origins, and encouraged by the new attitude to education that descended upon Europe with the Reformation, Erasmus and Dr Murner, cards became an instrument of schooling as well as a vehicle of excitement and greed, and in that capacity reversed their original role, cards becoming travellers rather than games.

In 1603, Andream Strobl of Sulzbach, in Bavaria, designed a thirty-two-card pack intended to help in the teaching of religious knowledge. Published in book form with copious notes, each of the cards, which were divided into the normal German suits, showed a Biblical scene and a suit sign. Issued under the title of *Das Geistliche Deutsche Carten Spil* they were commended by the Church. Strobl was followed by a Nuremberg publisher who produced, in 1640, a geographical pack with French suit signs.

In 1631 Johannes Amos Comenius, or Komenski, a Moravian scholar and educational reformer, published the first of the series of educational books which was to make his name known throughout Europe. Entitled *Janua Linguarum Reserata*, and written in Bohemian and Latin, it created such a stir in the world that it was translated into most European, and some Oriental, languages. In this book Comenius describes a method of teaching languages to children by means of things seen through the eye and heard through the ear, rather than through books of dry and remote learning. Twenty-seven years and a good many books later Comenius published *Orbis Sensualium Pictus*, a sort of picture book of the actual world, intended for the instruction of children. Perhaps his best known work, it was said to be the first of its kind. It is impossible to believe that these books were neither noticed nor read by Guilio Mazzarini, who, though never an ordained priest, was to achieve great eminence as Cardinal Mazarin, French Minister of State. A fanatical card-player, and according to some an equally fanatical card-sharper, he used cards for instructing his royal pupil.

In 1643 Louis XIV succeeded his father as King of France, and since he was under age his mother, Anne of Austria, became Regent. She relinquished affairs of state into the strong hands of His Eminence. As Superintendent of the King's education, Mazarin appointed a history master, a drawing master, an Italian master, a Spanish master, a guitar master and a lute master; and to ensure that no effort was spared to provide the king with a thorough education he caused four packs of educational cards to be prepared, mainly for the assistance of the principal teacher, Hardouin Péréfixe, the historian. The task of deciding on the details and the layout were entrusted to Jean Desmarests, Sieur de Saint-Sorlin, prominent man of letters, Councillor of the king, friend of Mazarin and holder of several public offices.

Beautifully engraved by the noted Florentine Stefano della Bella (known in France as Etienne de la Belle), the packs were listed as *Les Jeux de Cartes, des Roys de France, des Reines Renommées, de la Géographie, et des Fables*. Each card has a suit-sign and, according to the game, a picture of anything up to five kings, a queen or two, a symbolic figure (géographie) or a vignette illustrating a myth. Beneath each drawing is a short descriptive legend. To each of these queens is ascribed a virtue or a vice given in one word at the top of the card—brave, wise, unchaste, saintly and so on. Later the packs were bound together into a small book together with an Avis au Lecteur by the Sieur de Saint-Sorlin. The Sieur remarks that the cards were put together in a portable volume for the very easy learning of history, geography and the fables. In an address 'à la Reyne Régente' he says that 'it would appear that I am offering games to your Majesty, but in fact it is a book and a study for the young Princes at least as serious as it is entertaining. Here is a new Art created by a passionate desire to serve my King after having considered his beautiful and generous leanings.'

Anne of Austria, as could scarcely fail to be the case, is found to be among the famous queens. She takes the part of the king of clubs. The descriptive adjective at the top is 'saintly', and the text reads 'Queen of France, saintly, wise, of a marvellous goodness and of a modesty equal to her dignity . . . and Mother of a King given from Heaven at her desires who will surpass all the kings of the world.' Letters Patent granting Desmarests a monopoly in the sale of the cards were issued in 1644: and since the demand was so high that the packs had to be reprinted several times during the century this monopoly must have been profitable.

Following the publication of *Orbis Sensualium Pictus*, educational packs were now springing up in all directions. Heraldry, of immense importance on shields for the identification of documents, was an essential part of the education of princes, knights and gentlemen, and as such became the main interest of card-makers bent on deriving profit.

In 1655, Claude Oronce Finé, dit de Brianville, another Councillor of the king and also the Royal Almoner, designed a pack of cards to

Four cards from a Scottish book on heraldry, 1693. British Museum assist in the teaching of heraldry. It was called *Le Jeu D'Armoiries des Souverains et Estats d'Europe* and was published in Lyons. The layout is the same as that of the Desmarests cards, that is to say that they have a drawing of the subject of the lesson, in this case a coat of arms, in the upper part, with a written description, or blazonment, in the lower. There is a suit-sign in the top left-hand corner, and the aces are called cavaliers. To spades falls the honour of illustrating the coats of German and Scandinavian armigerous families; hearts, those of France; diamonds, those of Spain and Portugal; and clubs, those of Italy. Since at least fifteen editions of this pack are known, including an Italian edition produced at Naples by a French bookseller, Antony Bulifon, at whose home a society of young men calling themselves Academici Armoristi met weekly, it clearly met a need. The idea of teaching heraldry in this way was much flattered by imitation.

Richard Blome, a London publisher of some note, issued a pack in 1675 in which the armorial bearings of the different social grades were illustrated on the king, queen, and 10 to 3 of hearts. The ace and 2 displayed 'Military Things' and the knave 'Naval Things'. For this purpose Blome selected King Charles II, the Duke of Albemarle, the Earl of Bridgewater, the Viscount Kilmorey, Lord Berkeley, Sir Philip Matthews Bart, Sir John Drinkwater Kt., Thomas Barrington Esq. and Catharine Sedley. The Duke of Albemarle was the famous General Monk who restored Charles II to his throne. The remainder of the pack was devoted to an explanation of the various charges used in blazonry. But as a contemporary writer, Wood, says of Blome that he practised 'divers progging tricks' and adds that 'this person Blome is esteemed by the chiefest heralds a most impudent person, and the late industrious Garter hath told me that he gets a livelihood by bold practises'.

The Arms of the English Peers, issued in 1677 and reissued in 1684, 1686 and 1688, reverted to the original idea of showing individual coats, though with more than one shield to a card. It was 'printed for John Nicholson and sold by E. Evatts at the Green Dragon in St Paul's Churchyard', according to an advertisement in the *Observator*. In 1682 the Doge and Senate of Venice were presented with a pack by D. Casimir Franchet, Religieux Benedictin, who followed the de Brianville style. Called *Preggi della Nobilita Veneta*, the pack had violets, roses, lilies and tulips for suits. In 1691, a pack, for a long time now exceptionally rare, appeared in Edinburgh. Printed from plates engraved by a local goldsmith, Walter Scott, and coloured by hand, the full title of the pack is *The Blazoning of the Ensignes Armorial of the Kingdoms of Scotland, France and Ireland and of the coats of arms of the Nobility of Scotland. As they are illustrated upon the Cards Armorial.* In 1692 *Le Jeu de Cartes de Blason contenant les Armes des Princes des principales parties de l'Europe par Père C. F. Menestrier* was issued by Thomas Almaury of Lyons, the suits in this case being roses, lions, eagles and fleur-de-lis. When issuing his pack some forty years earlier, de Brianville paid tribute to the help he had received from Père Menestrier, made reference to the book the latter was preparing, and ended with a tribute to his vast capacity in the beautiful science. In his life-time Père Menestrier published many books on heraldry, the first in 1661, or six years after de Brianville's cards appeared.

Other heraldic packs were published: one in Nuremberg in 1693 and not unlike de Brianville's with arms of the reigning families of Europe; a *Jeu Heraldique* issued in Paris by Daumont and re-issued in Augsburg in 1698; and *Silvestre's Heraldry* printed in Paris in 1698, which was copied in Augsburg with German texts added, had a second German edition with the drawings in reverse which made nonsense of the heraldry, and was re-issued by Daumont in 1700.

If heraldry were the main stock in trade of the educational card seller, packs on quite a number of other subjects were to be found on his shelves. One, for instance, was military science, of importance, like heraldry, to the knight and his squire, which could be studied in *Le Jeu de la Guerre* and *Le Jeu des Fortifications*. Both packs followed the standard layout of having a suit sign in an upper corner, a drawing of the subject of the lesson in the top half of the card and an explanatory text in the lower half. Both had German editions and the *Jeu des Fortifications* a Spanish one as well. The German edition, known as *Das Festung Baues*, had an extra card showing the 'Complete Vestung' and for some unknown reason had the words printed in the top half of the card and the picture printed in the lower.

In the more ordinary fields, a knowledge of astronomy, geography, history, mathematics, grammar and carving could also be acquired through cards. Astronomy was provided for by a pack published in Nuremberg in 1656, which showed the orbits of the sun, moon, earth, and some of the planets; and by a second issued in London in 1676. The latter pack was by James Moxon, Hydrographer Royal, Fellow of the Royal Society, author of *Mechanic Exercises*, *Tutor to Astronomy and Geography* and other works. He then put out another publication entitled, *The Use of the Astronomical Playing Cards, Teaching any ordinary Capacity by them to be acquainted with all the stars in Heaven, to know their places in Heaven, Colour, Nature and Bigness. As also the Poetical Reasons for every Constellatio, Very Useful, Pleasant and Delightful for all Lovers of Ingeniety.* Moxon had his place of business at The Sign of the Atlas in Cornhill.

Geography was catered for more generously, especially as the Desmarests pack was in use until the end of the century. Three splendid English packs were published, in c. 1665, 1675 and in 1676, followed by three French packs, in 1669, 1675 and in 1684, and two German, the later in 1678. The first English pack was chiefly of value to a student for its text, the vignettes and figures at the tops of the cards were purely symbolical. The cards have the unusual feature of a second suit mark, in the case of spades a crescent moon (waxing), of hearts a Tudor rose, of diamonds a sun and of clubs a star. This was the work of H. Win-

See colour illustration page 48

From a seventeenth-century educational pack on Latin grammar.
British Museum

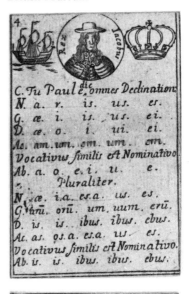

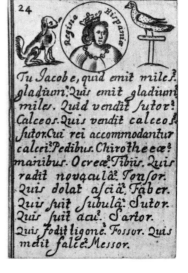

75

stanley of Littlebury in Essex, as we know from the inscription on the ace of hearts.

The second English pack was issued by Robert Morden, a geographer. In 1703 he was in business at the Sign of the Atlas in Cornhill, which, presumably, he bought on the death of James Moxon in 1700. These cards offered the geography student maps of all the fifty-two counties of England and Wales, together with some measurements entered at the bottom of the card. Among these were the 'Reputed and then the Measured Miles by Esqre Ogilby, with his leave incerted' of the distance of the county town from London. John Ogilby had established a publishing business in London where he produced maps and road books. In this pack the kings and queens are represented by busts of King Charles II and his queen Catharine of Braganza and the knaves by unidentifiable, but obviously humbler, persons. The third pack, published in 1676 by W. Redmayne, had small maps and large texts and it also dealt with the English counties. It was not very successful and is now rare.

In the French pack, which at different times appeared also in England, Germany and Italy, the suit of spades deals with Africa, hearts with Europe, diamonds with Asia and clubs with America. These cards also 'show the Longitude and Latitude of every part of the world; the Number of Kingdoms, Countries, Provinces and other Divisions; laid out by the celebrated Geographer, Monsieur Sanson'. It is claimed for Nicholas Sanson that he was the founder of the science of geography in France. The other two packs were *Le Jeu des Nations* published in 1684 and *Les Tables De Geographie* issued by P. Duval of Paris in 1669.

The two German packs were both published in Nuremberg, one pack, called *Typhus Orbis Terrarum*, dealing with different parts of the world, and the other with the countries of Europe, which included such, to our ears, unlikely sounding places as Selandria and Geldria (Zeeland and Guelderland). Engraved by Wilhelm Pfann, printed by Johann Hoffmann and invented by Johann Pretorious, they are painstakingly drawn and filled with intricate detail. They are also engraved with great clarity and are a tribute not only to German thoroughness but also to the German mastery of the art and craft of printing.

Of the other subjects, history was limited in the seventeenth century to a German reprint of *Les Reines Renommées* with a German text and German suit signs, and *Le Jeu Des Princes de l'Empire D'Allemagne* published by Pierre Duval in 1677. 'Scientall Cards' for 'acquiring without much labour but with much delight and profit the Rudiments of so necessary an art as grammar' were sold in London as early as 1651 and 'Grammatical Cards, comprizing the general rules of Lily's Grammar, in the four principal parts thereof, viz. Orthographia, Etymologia, Syntaxis, Prosodia', which were explained on spades, clubs, hearts and diamonds respectively, appeared in 1676. They were made by John Seller, another Royal Hydrographer and publisher

Cards from French
geographical packs.
Bowes Museum, Durham

76

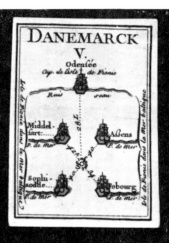

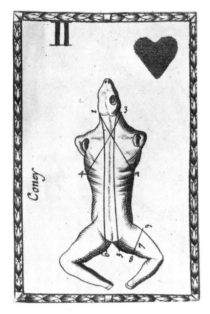

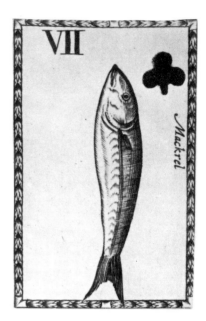

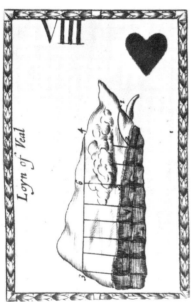

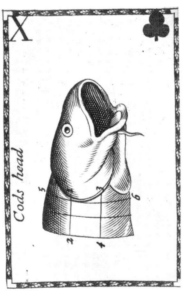

Carving cards with Lenthall border: 'All the Flesh of Beasts are rang among ye Suit of Hearts . . . all the Fish among the Suit of Clubs.' Bodleian Library, Oxford

and seller of maps, charts, and geographical books. James Moxon was responsible, in 1677, for the introduction of cards giving instruction in carving and, in 1697, posthumously, geometrical cards. The first showed 'the best manner of cutting up all sorts of wild and tame Fowl, Fish and Flesh', while the second, as the title says, has 'full and plain Instructions for the speedy attainment of that most useful and curious Science; with a printed Book of their use: Likewise, a Discourse of the

Mechanik Powers. All contrived by the late ingenious Mr Moxon.' Finally, there were a number of packs which fit into no category but make up a sort of cartological potpourri. Three of them were *The Scolers Practicall Cards*, which covered spelling, writing, ciphering, and casting up of accounts, and was placed on the market in 1656 by F. Jackson MA; a mathematical pack with the following announcement on the king of clubs: 'These cards, globes, spheres, mathematical Books, and instruments for Sea and Land, with many other curiosities in Gold, Silver, Steel, Brass, Ivory and Wood, and the best Charts, Maps, and Prints are sold at ye King's Armes and Globes at Charing Cross, and against the Royal Exchange in Cornhill, by Tho. Tuttell, Mathematical instrument maker to the King's most excellent Majesty, where are taught all parts of the Mathematics.' There was also a German pack of 'famous personages', printed at Augsburg by Johann Strindberg, offered to the undergraduates of the 'University of the Pack' in 1685.

While educational packs were pouring from the presses of Europe, England gave this type of card a new twist, initiating a variation upon a theme. Her card masters were the first to publish political propaganda and satirical packs, both of which had a considerable vogue, both in England and abroad, for a long time. But before we get involved with them we must first trace the remainder of the European story of cards, and then their history in England.

Cards in Switzerland, Poland, Scandinavia and the Low Countries

In the fourteenth century the Swiss military forces were the most formidable in Europe. With the feeling for independence given to the Confederation by a string of military victories, added to the example of William Tell in the previous century, it could never have been likely that any section of these hardy mountain people would follow tamely in the footsteps of their Italian or German counterparts. The Swiss card masters were no exception; and it is exceedingly interesting to note that they did not create entirely fresh designs. They introduced two entirely new suit marks, substituting shields and roses for hearts and leaves; but they retained the acorns and bells and the old German fluttering standard, though they used the latter for the aces instead of the tens. One cannot help wondering if half-measures only were adopted because the Swiss, despite being independent minded, wished to retain a link, however tenuous, with their German past.

It is not only in suit signs that the Swiss showed independent thinking: their court cards are distinctive. The king of shields has the unique distinction of having a baldachin over his head. He grasps a goblet in his right hand and beckons with his left, perhaps to his *unter* who is hurrying away with a letter in his right hand, a shield in his left, and a quill, not in a pen case, not even behind his ear, but in, of all places, his mouth. One receives the impression that the king wishes to make some alteration to his letter, presumably addressed to one of his fellow monarchs. The bearded king of acorns sits in a stately chair rather than on a throne and sometimes has the star of an order of chivalry on his chest and a radiant sun on the side of his chair; while the king of roses sometimes sits on a large throne and sometimes stands in front of a balustrade. The crowns of the kings of cups and bells are normally completed with a flower design while those of roses and acorns have small orbs. The stocking caps of the knaves end with a tassle, except for the *ober* of shields who is bareheaded. Otherwise the *obers* of acorns and bells smoke pipes, and the *ober* of shields has a hand in his pocket, all of which seems scarcely respectful at court; and the *unter* of bells has a circular head with flames sprouting from it, reminiscent of crude drawings of the sun, and holds in his right hand an indistinguishable object which is probably meant to be a stylus. In some packs the chevalier of swords is shown wearing a pauldron in the form of an upward-looking face exactly like those on the charioteer in the seventh trump of the tarot. In the eighteenth-century tarot packs, the Pope and Popess are often replaced by Jupiter and Juno. Each court card has its title printed in large capital letters at the foot.

Although many packs were printed in Switzerland, at Schaffhausen in the northeast, where the packs consisted of forty-eight cards—the twos were omitted—at Soleure in the northwest, where the packs had but thirty-six cards—the threes, fours, and fives being left out in addition to the twos—and also at Geneva, Fribourg, Neuchâtel, Basle, Mumlisweil and Unterwalden, many more were imported into the country from France, chiefly from Lyons and Rouen. As a result of a royal edict in 1583, many Lyonnaise card masters left their homeland and settled in Switzerland, though fifteen years later we hear of cards being specially manufactured in Lyons for the Swiss

Double-ended trump cards of standard Austrian pattern, c. 1880.
Collection Evelyn Goshawk; photo Peter Kibbles

Nineteenth-century Austrian
cards showing Oriental scenes,
suggesting travel and
exploration. By Piatnik,
Vienna.
Collection Evelyn Goshawk;
photo Peter Kibbles

market. Did the emigrants turn round and become immigrants as soon
as the edict, the revocation of which followed hard upon its imposition,
was repealed? That the Rouen trade with Switzerland was also large
is known from a petition of the card masters of that city against the
high excise duties levied on their products.

While other European countries have printed very attractive cards,
often with distinctive characteristics, none of those others has made
any original contribution to the basic conception. In the thirteenth and
fourteenth centuries many Germans flocked into Poland following in
the footsteps of the Teutonic knights, who were allowed to settle there
in 1226. That influx is reflected in Polish cards which are hybrid,
having the German sequence of king, *ober* and *unter* grafted upon the
Italian stock of swords, cups, coins and batons. There is in the Schreiber
collection (now in the British Museum) a most interesting thirty-six-
card pack made by J. G. Dupont of Warsaw in the eighteenth century.
Some of the courts bear such an astonishing resemblance to those in a
tarot pack made by J. Galler of Brussels, also in the eighteenth century,

OTAKAR II.

JAROSLAV

VÁCLAV IV.

JAN ŽIŽKA

BUDOVEC Z BUDOVA

ČECH

PROKOP HOLÝ

SLEZAN

X

that one can only suppose that J. G. Dupont was originally a Fleming. The Fleming pack has two unusual trumps. In the fifth the Pope is replaced by Bacchus sitting astride a barrel, a girdle of vine leaves and bunches of grapes round his waist and a bottle at his lips. The Popess is replaced by 'L'Espagnol, Capitaine Eracasse', a dashing character in ruff and high hat with a sword across his hip. These same two trumps also appear in two other packs of the same period, one printed by F. I. Vandeboore of Brussels and another by John Gisaine of Dinant-sur-Meuse.

At first the Scandinavian market was a German preserve. It became lost to Germany during the course of the Thirty Years War (1618–48), when the Hapsburgs tried to add the Baltic Ports to the Austrian Empire, when Tilly and Wallenstein, each with his own army swept over northern Germany, only to be defeated—and in the case of Tilly mortally wounded—by Gustavus Adolphus of Sweden. Scandinavia then became a French market, and the card masters of Rouen, who in 1701 claimed such large exports to Switzerland, asserted at the same time that they did a brisk trade with Sweden and Denmark. Although the cards have the French suit signs to this day, the courts, which have a distinctive, blonde, northern charm of their own, are named after Swedish, not French, heroes, such as Gustafvasa, otherwise Gustavus I, the liberator and founder of the royal line, Gustavus II, otherwise Gustavus Adolphus, and Carl II, a warrior king with all the virtues of a hardy soldier and victor in many battles.

Though they made no changes in the suit marks or the designs of the court cards, the Low Countries were among the first to set up in the card manufacturing business. The year 1379, in which the Duke of Brabant purchased several packs of *speelquarten*, was only a couple of years after Johannes' sermon. And Henry d'Allemagne, author of the vast *Cartes à Jouer du XIVe au XXe Siècle*, was of the opinion that the cards which so worried the police of Lille in 1382 came from across the Belgian border. In neither cases are there any clues as to the kind of cards involved; but at that early date, and with the Low Countries under the heel of Spain, we must suppose that the cards were of the Italo/Spanish type. There is evidence to show that both French and Spanish type cards were in use in the first quarter of the sixteenth century; and it is surely reasonable to presume that Spanish cards were entirely rejected, and French fully accepted, when, to quote Motley's Dutch Republic, 'the most sublime sentence of death was promulgated which has ever been pronounced since the creation of the world . . .'.

Upon the 16th of February, 1568, a sentence of the Holy Office condemned all the inhabitants of the Netherlands to death as heretics. From the universal doom only a few persons, especially named, were excepted. A proclamation of the king, dated ten days later, confirmed the decree of the Inquisition, and ordered it to be carried into execution without regard to age, sex or condition. This

Czechoslovakian pack depicting national heroes. Suits are bells, hearts, acorns and leaves. Collection Evelyn Goshawk; photo Peter Kibbles

85

is the most concise death warrant that was ever framed. Three millions of people, women and children, were sentenced to the scaffold in three lines.

These appalling events led to the resistance of the Wild Beggars, from whom sprang the Sea Beggars, who captured the city of Brill in 1572 and put in train the overthrow of the Spanish dominion over the Netherlands. Surely we can safely presume that the same events would also have resulted in the final rejection of Spanish type cards and, once England had started the fashion of propaganda and political packs, in the inspiration behind one of the bitterest antipapal packs.

Cards were manufactured in all the large cities of Belgium— Tournai, Antwerp, Brussels, Liège, Ghent, Bruges, Namur, Dinant, Charleroi, Ypres, Nieuport, Mons and Ostend to mention but some of them. Tournai is believed to have been the first town to have engaged in the industry. There were at least two card masters there as early as 1427, Michel Noël and Phillips du Bos, and the chances are that they were not the first. As time passed, many French card masters, driven from France by high taxation, emigrated to Belgium in the same way that their counterparts left Lyons for Switzerland. The cards that these masters produced tended to be on the large side, with the kings, and queens, and knaves in proportion.

In Holland (it was in 1578 that Belgium and Holland decided to go their separate ways) Amsterdam became the centre of the card manufacturing industry, among the early masters being the partner- ship of J. Covens and Mortier, who established themselves in the seventeenth century, and whose business was particularly well known, both at home and abroad, for its educational and other speciality cards, mostly reproductions of French packs.

About 1670 an unidentified printer published a pack of cards designed to teach Latin grammar. The suit of each card was indicated by a single sign in the middle of the bottom margin and the value shown by the number of special symbols set out in the ordinary way. The symbols appropriated to the suit of hearts were shields; to spades, bunches of grapes; to diamonds, quatrefoils; and to clubs, marigolds. The text of the lessons was printed on the special symbols. The court cards had fanciful, full length figures.

Among Mortier packs were *Le Jeu de Boufon*, published about 1690; *Le Jeu de quatre parties du Monde*, *Le Jeues Hommes et Femmes Illustres* and *Le Jeu des Rois de France*, all published about 1700; and *Le Jeu des Metamorphoses d'Ovide* published *c.* 1705.

Le Jeu de Boufon was printed in red ink and the cards were small, $2\frac{1}{4} \times 1\frac{1}{4}$ inches. In the top half of each card there was a circle with the portrait of a buffoon, sometimes head and shoulders and sometimes three quarters length. In the lower half was a miniature card which had to be printed sideways in order to fit it in, and over the top was the name of the buffoon. The 9 of spades, for example, shows a grinning

English mythological cards 'sold only at Willerton's Toy Shop in Bond Street'; a reversed facsimile of a French pack, Mortier's *Jeu des Métamorphoses d'Ovide*. Bodleian Library, Oxford

86

MOMUS

was the Harliquin of Heaven,

turning into ridicule, the

Actions, both of Gods & Men.

ARACHNE

was a Princess admirably Skilld
in Tapestry Work, till becoming
too vain of her Talent, She had
the Presumption, to challenge
Minerva, who accepted the Defy,
but seeing the Work of Arachne
nearly as Beautiful as her own,
She was so invitated, that she
transform'd her into a Spider.

The SYRENS

were the Daughters of the River God
Achelous, they beg'd of the Gods that
they might take the form of Birds, that
they might the more effectually seek
after Proserpine, their dear Companion
whom Pluto had convey'd to the Infernal
Regions, they obtain'd their wish, at
the same time reserving the Faces
of women.

CHARON

the ferryman of Hell, carried
the Souls of the Dead over the
three Rivers Acheron, Stix & Cocytus,
every one that enter'd his Boat,
was oblig'd to give him a Piece
of Money, he is represented in a
crazy Boat, very Old & Ragged.

hunchback called Esopus; the 9 of hearts has a three-quarter length figure of a man called Chapin, who has a goose-like face under a flat cap and above a pointed beard jutting aggressively forward; and the ace of clubs is Koele Jacob drawn as a clown. The courts are full length with the name at the bottom.

Le Jeu de quatre parties du Monde had delicate, allegorical figures with a line of text at the bottom of the card and was engraved by the well known Dutch artist Jacob Gole, who, professionally at least, moved in royal circles. Line engravings of the King of Sweden, the Sultan of Turkey, and mezzotints of the King of Spain and the King of Poland were among his work. The figures in the pack represented the four quarters of the world (the tens of each suit standing for America, Africa, Asia and Europe), the four seasons of the year (the queens posing for spring, summer, autumn and winter), the four divisions of the day (the eights represent morning, midday, afternoon and night); the twelve months, the elements, the seasons; and various arts and sciences, such as painting, printing, astrology, oratory and medicine.

Le Jeu des Hommes et Femmes Illustres had heads of the illustrious in the top half of the card with an account of them in the lower. They included Plato, Solon, Virgil, Sappho, Zenobia and Areta. *Le Jeu des Rois de France*, also engraved by Gole, had two heads at the top of each card, below which were about nine lines of text for each head, excepting the courts which were full length figures with three or four lines of French to proclaim their fame. They differed, however, in one particular from other packs by having their value shown by a miniature card printed at their side.

Le Jeu des Metamorphoses d'Ovide, yet a third example of Gole's work, followed the same principle as the others with the difference that some of the characters need more than one card to tell their story. Jupiter, for instance, needs the 2, 3, 6 and queen of hearts; and Neptune the 2, 10 and queen of diamonds. Among the lesser known figures is La nimphe Salmacia, who is pictured under a tree on a river bank. The text reads:

Ayant vu le Jeune Hermaphrodite elle en devint amoreuse, et layant surpris qui se baignoit, elle seietta dans leau, le retint par force, et pria les Dieux de changer leurs deux corps enyn seul, ce qui lui fut accordé.

[Having seen the young Hermaphrodite she fell in love with him, and having surprised him as he bathed, she threw herself into the water, held him back by force, and prayed the Gods to change their two bodies into one, which was granted to her.]

88

The excise duty on cards, having had the undesirable effect of driving French card masters abroad, was abolished in France in the seventeenth century; though not for long. For in 1701 the Government, faced with a Treasury severely straitened by war expenditure on the one hand and a revenue reduction, as a direct result of the expulsion of the Huguenots, who had carried on a large part of French industry, on the other, re-imposed the tax. The rate was fixed at 18 deniers a pack. Following the customary French administrative procedure of dividing the country into a number of tax regions (it was split into six for the *gabelle*, or salt duty, and a fluctuating number of *Généralités* for general tax purposes) the Controller-General of Finance established nine card tax regions. Each region was allotted its own card design, and the absolute duty of printing cards to the regional design was laid upon the manufacturers. Design blocks had to be deposited with the *Recettes générales*, or local Treasuries, or with the police. No doubt the Controller-General persuaded the card masters that a single design would bring economies of production and increases in profits; but a tax inspector who cares in the least for the tax-payer's welfare is as rare as a black snowdrop. In this case the sole aim of the Controller-General was to ease the work of his collectors and obtain the highest revenue. It was against this taxation that the card masters of Rouen appealed.

It must not be supposed that nine brand new patterns were now created. Far otherwise: for while there were distinct differences between some of the packs there were equally marked likenesses. It was almost, though not quite, as if the Controller-General had taken a standard design and told the card masters to rearrange its parts so as to make different wholes. In these regional patterns we find that first this king has a bird on this wrist and then that one, that among the queens the flowers and fans are shuttled around, while in the case of knaves now one has plaited hair and now another.

The nine designated regions were Paris, Bourgogne, Lyonnais, Auvergne, Dauphiné, Provence, Languedoc, Guyenne and Limousin; and they remained in being until repealed by the States General in the last decade of the century. Their characteristics were as follows:

Paris This region took in the whole of the north of France, including the towns of St Omer in the Pas de Calais, Rouen, Brest on the Finisterre peninsular jutting out into the Atlantic, Nantes on the western coast, Tours, Troyes and, to complete the circle, Lille. In 1751 the Controller added the cities of Epinal, Strasbourg on the German

Card wrapper by Guillaume Gautier from a French factory at Troyes. British Museum

CARTES TRES FINES

FAICTES A TROYES PAR GVILLAV
ME GAVTIER DEMEVRANT EN LA
RVE NOSTRE DAME A LENSEIGNE
DE LA TRVYE QVI IOVE AVX CARTES

frontier, Metz and Nancy.

Points in the Paris design, which was known in the seventeenth century, if not earlier, which immediately catch the eye are that the knave of clubs, usually called Lancelot, has no name though he carries that of the card master, and all the rest of the Court retain their names, and all have rather large bodies. Then, among the kings, hearts has an imperial eagle hidden in the folds of his cloak, clubs is accompanied by a small animal which might be a lion, diamonds has a shell-shaped panel let into his cloak on which is a fleur-de-lis, and spades leans against a harp. As for the queens, they wear crowns of fleur-de-lis design and hold a flower in one hand, and the queen of spades like the king of diamonds has a shell-like panel on her cloak; in addition the queen of clubs holds a fan in her left hand, while from 1751 the queen of diamonds carried in her left hand a bag embroidered with a 'thought'. The knave of diamonds is drawn in profile and the knave of hearts full face; both wear a jerkin reaching nearly to their knees, and their stockings are embroidered. They and the knave of clubs lean on a halberd; and the knave of spades, who wears a hat with a feather, is accompanied by his dog, which jumps against his left leg.

Bourgogne This district lay in the middle of France on the eastern side and took in the towns of Dijon, Besançon and Salins. The regional pattern is merely a 'crib' of that produced at Lyons in the seventeenth century and exported to Bourgogne, Lorraine, Provence and Flanders. The cards are small, making the figures appear rather squat; but the chief feature is the long, splendid plume flowing from the knave of

90

clubs' helmet, from which the pack acquired the name of *La Plume à Chapeau*. In this pattern the kings wear large floral crowns with, at the very least, five flowers apiece, voluminous robes trimmed with ermine and, except for the king of hearts, hold a sceptre decorated with a fleur-de-lis. In addition the king of hearts has a kind of ring on his chest. The queens, excepting the queen of diamonds, hold a flower and wear large embroidered cloaks. The knave of hearts is the only one seen full-face, and the knave of clubs, as in the Paris design, carries by a cord a shield for the display of the name and trademark of the card

Cards by P. Ressy, Paris, c. 1780, and by G.D., Paris (probably cards from two different, though similar, packs). The Jack of Clubs shows 'Aux Armes de Paris'. Bodleian Library, Oxford

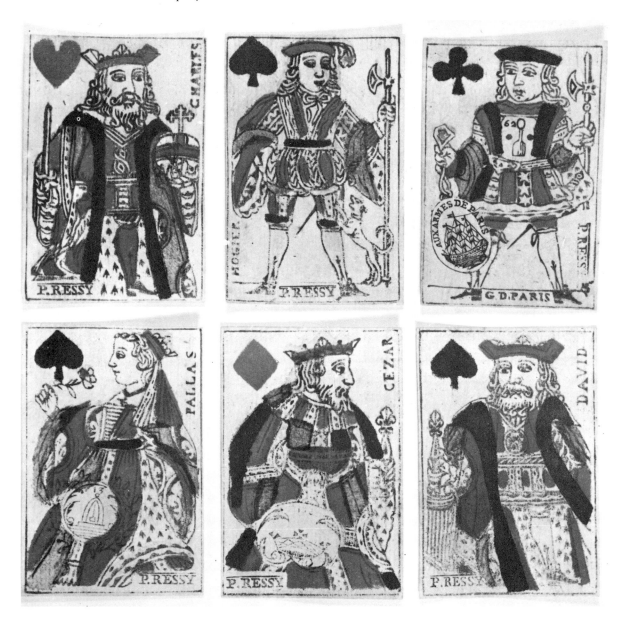

master. The knave of spades has his hair in plaits and the name of the town of origin printed on the card between his feet.

Lyonnais   The Lyonnais design was, basically, that used by the card masters of Lyons and the surrounding district in the sixteenth and early part of the seventeenth century. The four kings together with the queens of hearts and spades originally carried floral sceptres, the king of hearts a bird on his wrist, the queen of hearts a flower, and the queen of clubs nothing at all, though her card bore the inscription 'Mais Bien Vous'. The full-faced knave of clubs leant on a club, and the knave of spades wore a kind of visor and carried an axe on which the engraver incised his initials. In this precise form the pack is rare.

In 1711 the knave of spades had a pipe put in his mouth, for which one card master, Chavrot, substituted a rose; and five years later the queen of clubs lost her inscription. In 1751 the king of clubs had added an orb, and all the kings exchanged their floral sceptres for fleur-de-lis, spades carrying his over his left shoulder. The queens of hearts and spades have been deprived of their sceptres, and all four queens now carry a flower in one hand and a fan in the other. The knave of clubs has been given a tricorne, his club has been replaced by a lance, and on his right arm he now has a shield: 'Lyon' is printed between his feet.

Auvergne   This district lay in central France and included the towns of Thiers, renowned far and wide for its card manufacture, Clermont and Le Puy. The design seems to be a replica of that used by the well known card master of Thiers in the previous century—Jean Volay. The kings of diamonds, spades and clubs carry sceptres which in the case of hearts is replaced by a sword, and the king of clubs has a parrot perched on his left hand. All the queens hold a sceptre with a flower or a fleur-de-lis on the top, while clubs, hearts and diamonds also carry a flower. In place of the flower the queen of spades has a small dog balanced on her right arm; her hair is caught up in a caul and her crown appears to be on the point of falling off. The knaves all wear armour, carry a sword and lean on a halberd; and the knave of hearts has a lyre-shaped badge representing arms, replaced by the lion of Thiers if from that city, in the middle of his breast-plate.

In the latter half of the eighteenth century the export of cards to Spain became of such importance to the card masters of Auvergne that they deposited a second design to be used in the export trade. Neighbouring provinces were included in this arrangement.

In this design the king of clubs and the queen of spades have lost their parrot and dog, and the king of hearts' sword has been replaced by a sceptre. The king of spades is now brandishing an axe. The queens have given up their sceptres and taken up flowers. The knave of clubs leans on a club with a heart on it carrying the designer's initials. The knave of spades is shown full face with his hand on his hip and with either the lion from the arms of Thiers, or part of a fleur-de-lis, embroidered on his chest. The knaves of hearts and diamonds are seen in half-profile.

Dauphiné   This district lay in the south east of the kingdom, bounded by the Alps, the Rhone and Provence. The principal towns engaged in card production were Grenoble, Romans and Valence. Unfortunately only a few cards in this design are extant; but from those that have survived it can be said that it is now the turn of the king of diamonds to have a bird on his wrist and of the knave of clubs to have his hand on his hip. The knave of diamonds, who is bareheaded and wrapped in a cloak, has faces stamped on the front of his boots, while the knave of hearts has a drawn sword in his right hand and points upwards with his left.

Provence   This district, the cradle of poetry and romance and the paradise of the troubadours, lies in the south east corner of France, the main card producing towns being Aix, Marseilles, Toulon, Avignon, Nîmes and Montpellier. The design is an ancient one (in the collection of the United States Playing Card Company there are examples dating from the fifteenth century) and is thought by M. d'Allemagne to have been based on that of the cards shipped to Provence from Lyons at an even earlier date. The king of hearts has a small bird perched on his wrist, and the bird, as well as the king, has both a crown and a human face: clubs is armed with an axe decorated with a fleur-de-lis; diamonds has an exceptionally thin sceptre surmounted by a flower; and spades, seen in profile, holds his sceptre over his shoulder. Among the queens is to be found one of the most distinctive characteristics of the early examples of this portrait: for Her Majesty of hearts wears what appear to be scales, but is, possibly, fur under her robe, which can also be seen on her arms and legs—in the latter case because she is holding up her skirt with her right hand. Leaning backwards, she balances on her left leg. The queens of clubs and spades hold flowers, and the queen of diamonds wears a curious, ring-like, fleur-de-lis trimmed tippet. She has, in the fifteenth-century cards, the charming motto of the card master, Francois Arnoux, 'Vive les bons enfants qui jouvent souvent', printed down the sides of her card. The knave of hearts is drawn full faced, stands with his right hand on his hip and holds his halberd with his left; both the knaves and clubs and spades have plaited hair, and the knave of diamonds has a jerkin reaching to his knees, as in the Paris design, and a curious sort of pleated head-dress on his head, possibly a capuchin.

Languedoc   This region was in the south of France, on the eastern side, and lies between the Garonne and the Rhone. The capital was Toulouse, and the regional design was published in that city and also in Carcassonne, Beziers and Albi. The 'portrait de Languedoc' is much similar to that of Auvergne, and to the following two, those of

Guyenne and Limousin: for these three are, really, reproductions of the Auvergne design. The most notable feature of the Languedoc portrait is the king of diamonds, who carries a purse in his right hand while he holds an orb in his left; and the second most noteworthy point is also to be found in the king of hearts who wears a breast-plate with a large fleur-de-lis on it. The town of Le Puy, in the Auvergne district, managed to establish a right to use the Languedoc design as well as that of Auvergne, presumably because of its geographical position.

Guyenne Guyenne, a word which is a corruption of Aquitania, occupies the western part of southern France together with the south-west corner, the chief towns being Bordeaux, Montauban and Agen. In this design the king of hearts is carrying a very thin sceptre, with a large fleur-de-lis at the top, while the king of clubs' sceptre ends with a heart-shaped ornament surmounted by a flaming vase. The king of diamonds, with a large cloak, holds in his right hand a pointed shield, upon it the arms of France, and in his left a sceptre topped by a heart-shaped ornament. Later in the century the arms of France were replaced by the monogram of Louis XIV and later still by a shining sun. The king of spades is the axe holder, and on his chest is a rose within a circle. All the knaves have large sleeves, but those of the knave of hearts are particularly voluminous. The knave of diamonds has a trim, pointed beard, and is the twin of his opposite number from Thiers. The knave of spades has his right hand on his hip, holds his halberd with his left and has the maker's name at one side; Agen always printed this knave wearing, on his chest, a picture of a fortress, with towers and dungeon, topped by a flame; and the knave of clubs plaited hair beneath a flat cap, and a flower and the name of the town of manufacture between his feet.

From Bordeaux many cards were shipped to Spain.

Limousin This region lay in the middle of France on the western side. Its design, which was a bad copy of the Auvergne design, was used by the cities of Limoges, Angoulême and Poitiers. Limoges also exported much of her production to Spain.

Faced by a determined Controller-General the French card masters complained of the burden of taxation; but they did not curtail, let alone abandon, their operations. Limoges, Bordeaux and Thiers, as we have seen, enjoyed a brisk business with Spain; Lyons traded with Switzerland; Rouen in her plea for mitigation of the tax, pointed out that 'the reputation of the cards of Rouen is known in Spain, Sweden, Russia, Switzerland, Denmark, England and especially Flanders'. 'Kings climb to eminence', says Austin Dobson, 'over men's graves'. And about 1780 the Paris pattern triumphed over the other portraits and became general throughout France. Cardboard kings also conquer at

Hector de Trois. Seventeenth-century French regional pack. Original pack in the Bibliothèque Nationale, Paris. Reproduced 1963 by French master-cardmakers including Camoin, Miro, Le Triboolet, Grimaud, Philibert. Photo Peter Kibbles

95

Named court cards from a
standard French pack by
Grimaud, 1890.
Collection Evelyn Goshawk;
photo Peter Kibbles

the expense of other men's profits, and in the first half, at least, of the
eighteenth century France was much occupied in consolidating and
extending her position in those markets which she had so successfully
snatched from Germany during the Thirty Years War. The tax,
incidentally, was abolished in 1719, re-introduced in 1751 when

96

Louis XV founded the Royal Military School and endowed it with a card tax, and suppressed in 1791, at the same time that an import duty was introduced.

Despite the competition, Germany continued to produce cards with intricate designs, her one concession to the French commercial attack lying in the use of French suit signs in some of her packs. Andreas Benedictus Gobl of Munich printed many packs in which the numbered cards displayed charming miniatures, in which a variety of tiny people followed a diversity of occupations, and the court cards were filled from the very top margin to the very bottom with ornately dressed figures. Many had German suits, some had hearts and diamonds, spades and clubs. Other card masters were Sebastian Foja and J. Albrecht of Augsburg; Lauretz Ummer, Joseph Fletcher and P. F. Ulrich of Munich; and masters with the monograms IS and ALS. Towards the end of the century Ulrich produced a pack of musical tarots in which the court cards had operatic figures instead of the usual kings and queens and knaves, and the trumps had opera music in place of the customary designs.

In the middle of the century a fashion developed in Germany for animal tarots in which strange creatures, without any particular significance, took the place of the Popess and the Hanging Man and the rest of the curious coterie. An example of this type of pack is one made by Gobl in which a wonderful array of bears, deer, monkeys, hares, leopards and other animals disport themselves, a many-coloured peacock plucks her breast to feed her young, like a pelican in her piety, and a unicorn swims in the sea past an island, with head erect and horn pointing to heaven, gulls circling overhead. Although these trumps seem devoid of meaning they possess much charm.

Unnamed court cards from a standard French pack by Grimaud, 1914 or earlier. Collection Evelyn Goshawk; photo Peter Kibbles

At the same time the spate of educational packs continued. Indeed, the work of the educational reformers, especially that of the great German educationalist Johann Bernhard Basedow (1723–90), must have encouraged the European card masters in general, and German in particular, to maintain their output of this type of card. The son of a Hamburg wigmaker, Johann was educated at the Gymnasium there and afterwards at Leipzig University. He then spent three years as tutor to a young boy, after which he sat for his master's degree for which he wrote a thesis on educational methods setting out his own views. Since he had, when a tutor, made much use of Comenius's *Orbis Pictus* there is little surprise in finding that Basedow's ideas are substantially those of Comenius. The disciple agreed with the master 'that all our knowledge begins with the senses', and his method was to make the acquisition of knowledge through play. In 1774 he published his *Elementwark* which was, really, another *Orbis Pictus* with one hundred copper-plate engravings by Chodowiecki, the Polish painter and engraver whose vignettes were so popular that hardly any artistic work of the period appeared without examples of his work. Basedow was followed by Pestalozzi, born about twenty years after him, who, making great play with the word 'Anschauung', said very much the same thing.

Following an heraldic pack in 1717, Germany produced two geographical packs, one a reproduction of the much copied M. Sanson's and the other a reproduction of the *Jeu de Géographie;* an astronomical pack in 1719, and an Old Testament pack which had four flower suits, yellow, red, blue, and green, with the number of the card at the top and under it a Biblical scene. Blaue V, for instance, shows a figure lying on an imposing bed with the bed-curtains drawn back, a paved floor, and an open end to the room beyond which one can see a tree, with a couple of birds perched in it, and several small animals grazing; beneath are four lines of text beginning 'Nebucadnetzar wird erschreckt Im Traum. . . .'. The calligraphic pack shows several kinds of script on the cards which also have figures of men and women, very strangely composed of the loops and twirls used by a calligraphic artist. The value of the card is indicated by a suit mark in the top left-hand corner of the card and a number in the top right.

Switching our attention from north to south, we find Italy, having put out a second edition of the Venetian heraldry in 1707, seized by a sudden thirst for geographical knowledge. This was evidenced first by still another copy of M. Sanson's *Jeu de Gégraphie*, offered for sale in 1717, which was followed by a geographical *tarocchino* pack printed in Bologna which for some unknown reason displeased the Pope. He insisted that trumps 2 to 5, that is the Popess and the Pope, the Empress and the Emperor, be withdrawn. They were replaced by Moors. These two packs were followed by *Giuoco Geografico dell'Eoropa*, brought out in 1770, in which the suits are *nord, sud, centro* and *isole*. The cards are numbered 1 to 13, and the ancient kingdom of Galloway is moved

Animal tarot by Johann
Mathus Sedlmayr, Augsburg
c. 1780.
Bodleian Library, Oxford

from Scotland to Ireland. Another pack issued in 1779 by Albrizzi of Venice (who in the same year printed a pack dealing with the history of the Popes) was devoted to world geography, the suit of swords coping with Africa, of cups with Europe, of money with Asia, and of batons with America; and finally by a tarot pack published in Parma in 1790 which has each card printed with *nord* at the top, *sud* at the bottom, and *est* and *ouest* at the sides.

Turning aside from geography, 1748 saw the production of a celebrated Italian pack. This was a sequence of Biblical cards with original drawings by Francesco Zuccarelli, an Italian painter who spent a good many years in England and was a founder member of the Royal Academy. In this pack the suit signs are orange circles, above which appears one of the letters of the alphabet from the sequence A to NN; pink hearts surmounted by the letters A to NN; yellow diamonds with the letters O to Z; and lavender jars with the letters O to Z. A drawing of an animal, a human being or some other design appears on the suit sign. The cards have vignettes of Biblical events, a typical one being the assumption of Elias the Tishbite, otherwise the Prophet Elijah into heaven. He is seen reclining in a chariot as he is carried up by a whirlwind. Five lines of text at the top, and again at the bottom, complete the card.

Spain's sole contribution to this wealth of learning was a copy of de Brainville's heraldry. Switzerland produced rather more, since in 1744 Rudolph Hauser of Geneva published the *Jeu d'Officiers*, an original conception which showed pictures of soldiers in the uniform of different European countries, some very wild and fierce looking, some mild in appearance, and some with women. Shortly afterwards the *Nouveau Jeu d'Officiers en LII figures en Habit de Guerre*, in which the court cards of the first pack were replaced by additional officers, was produced by the same publisher. In each case the figures were selected from a series of 151 engraved by Martin Englebrecht who, with his brother Christian, ran a printsellers and engravers business in Augsburg. In 1760 France added her portion of knowledge, contained in a number of *Jeux des Cartes Historiques* (Grecian, Roman and Ancient) put out by Vanackers of Lille, in which a woodcut portrait by E. Jouey of a famous character, such as Homer or Semiramis, appears at the top of each card, the rest of the available space being taken up with a letterpress biography. At the close of the century a pack for teaching English and Portuguese to Frenchmen made its appearance. It was poorly printed and the English was not the language Shakespeare spoke nor the French that of the Academy. French card masters of the eighteenth century may not have taken a very active part in the dissemination of knowledge through playing cards; but in the latter part of the century at least they were certainly busy in other directions.

Towards the end of the period a copy of Count de Gebelin's book *Le Jeu des Tarots, ou l'on traite de son origine ou on explique des Allegories & ou l'on fait voir qu'l est la source des nos cartes modernes à jouer* fell into the hands of a somewhat credulous Paris wigmaker called Alliette. Immensely impressed by de Gebelin's theory that the tarot was nothing less than a secret edition of the ancient Egyptian book of Thoth as well as by the mysticism and symbolism to be found in the work, he was quite overcome at the discovery that the passing years had spared a book which was' composed in the 1828 year of Creation, or 171 years after the Deluge, and written 3953 years ago by 17 Magi, including Athodis, a descendant of Mercury who was also a grandson of Ham and therefore a great-grandson of Noah'. Alliette promptly became immersed in a study of a variety of arcane subjects such as numerology, a study which led him to claim that fortunes could be told by means of cards. In 1783 he published a book entitled *Manière de se recréer avec Le Jeu de Cartes nommées Tarots*, after which he proceeded to design his own prophetic packs, taking pains to have them printed under the pseudonym of Etteilla (a reversal of his own name).

These packs came in several designs and editions. The thirty-six-card packs were smaller than most, and had charmingly engraved figures, a number in the top right-hand corner, and a 'fortune' printed across the top of the card with an illustration beneath. Thus in one pack No 12 has 'Bon Voyage par mer' at the top with a picture of a three masted sailing ship below. In the bottom of the right-hand corner is either the representation of a small card or a box containing the message 'Consultant, Etteila' or 'Consultant pour la reussite Etteila' or some similar message. The tarot packs are not so felicitously printed. Some of the trumps retain the flavour, if not the essence, of the original designs. No 14, for instance, is named *le diable* and depicts a winged being standing on a short pillar to which a man and woman are chained, a design which closely resembles that of the original trump No XIV. The 'fortune' in this case is 'Force Majeure' when the card is the right way up and 'Force Mineure' when it is upside down. These cards had a great success and Etteilla claimed many distinguished followers—it was even hinted that Napoleon was among them, a hint which the little wigmaker would certainly encourage. Reward or not, Etteilla became widely known and attracted not only followers but rivals, some of whose cards were more or less a direct copy of the master's.

With the Revolution, the printed princes suffered no less than those of flesh and blood. Louis XVI and Marie Antoinette lost their heads. David and Caesar, Judith and Rachel, and the rest of the cardboard rulers lost their royal insignia, and finally received sentence of banishment. The card masters were assured by two of their number, Urbaine Jaume and Jean Demosthene Dugoure, writing in the *Journal de Paris*, that the signs and insignia of monarchy were offensive to any good Republican, and as an immediate response to that advice saw to it that their copper plates or wood blocks were lowered at the points where offending emblems were engraved, so that nothing of that part could be printed. If a crown on its own were removed, and no other action was taken, the unfortunate monarch faced the world not only crownless but scalpless. In some cases the problem was met by painting in a cap of liberty. After the first hasty adjustment to a revolutionary society, the court figures were themselves banished, by a decree dated 22 October 1793, being replaced by *genies* (*coeur* being the genius of war), *trèfle* of peace, *pique* of arts and *carreaux* of commerce, *libertés* and *egalitiés* and other symbols which did not clash with Jacobin principles.

There are few records of the infancy of playing cards in England. An act of Parliament, dated 1463, prohibiting 'after the feast of St Michael the Archangel next coming' the importation of a variety of 'wares or chaffers' ranging from 'firetongs, dripping-pans, dice and tennis balls' through 'playing cards, pins, pattins, pack needles and painted wares' to 'cards for wool and blanch iron thread commonly called White Wire'. Chaucer, who died in 1400, had a large experience of life and must have met cards were they there to be met. His *Canterbury Tales* fully reflect English life of the period, and yet there is no mention of card playing. We can conclude that cards reached England somewhere between 1400 and 1463.

Turning our gaze towards the source and design of the first English cards, the first light comes from the fact that to this day we speak of spades and clubs rather than *piques* and *trèfles* or pikes and clover, a pointer to the first cards being of Spanish or Italian design. That being so, then they must have been imported from France before the invention of the French suit marks around 1430, or from Spain or Italy direct, or from the Low Countries which were still under Spanish dominion and, presumably, using Spanish type cards.

The state of French trade at the vital period seems to preclude the first possibility. The Hundred Years War, which raged from 1382 to 1453 disrupted French commerce and industrial development. The Italian merchants who normally conducted much of their export business at the great French fairs now followed the Genoese and Venetians in sailing direct to the Channel ports. The control of the sea lanes passed from the French to the Spanish and Portuguese. The great French towns diminished and the workmen, to escape starvation, emigrated. Certainly France began to recover before the Hundred Years War was over; but not in time to carry on any sort of flourishing export trade in the first quarter of the century.

W. A. Chatto, author of *Facts and Speculations on the Origins and History of Playing Cards*, published in 1848, raises upon a wafer-thin foundation the suggestion that cards reached England from Ireland and Ireland from Spain. He bases this opinion on a sentence in Edmund Spenser's *View of the Present State of Ireland*. 'Next to this', writes Spenser, speaking of certain lewd classes in Ireland, 'this' being a 'frye of rakehelle horseboys',

there is another much like, but much more leude and dishonest; and that is, of theyre Kearroghs, which are a kind of people that wander up and downe to genetellmens howses, living onely upon cardes and dice, the which though they have litle or nothing of theyr owne, yet will they play for much money, which yf they winne, they waste most lightlie, and if they loose, they paie as slenderlie, but recompense with one stealth or another, whose only hurt is not, that they themselves are idle lossels, but that through gaming they drawe others to like lewdness and idleness.

Spain, says Mr Chatto, had the same sort of 'idle lossels', and he therefore sees that country as the one from which cards first reached Ireland, and, he implies, the British Isles. When we consider the Low Countries, we have noted that cards were known in Belgium at least as early as 1379, and before the end of the century whole barrel loads were being exported to England. Usually the maker's name was omitted from these packs, though that of the English customer, and sometimes the manufacturer's trademark, such as a rose or wild boar, appeared on one of the cards. The reason for this arrangement was that England enjoyed a very brisk export trade with Spain; and though we are now speaking of sixty or seventy years later than the vital period it seems hardly likely that English export trade at the end of the century was founded upon a slender import trade at the beginning, especially as Spain was never a great card manufacturing country and obtained most of its supplies by importation. By and large, the Low Countries seem to be the likeliest source of the original English cards.

Whatever the beginnings, in the last quarter of the century playing cards are mentioned in more than one record; in an Act forbidding their import into the kingdom in 1463 for one; in the *Paston Letters* for Christmas Eve 1483 for another; in the private accounts of Henry VII for a third; and in a prohibition, issued in 1495, of their use by servants and apprentices at Christmastide for a fourth. But the first mention of an actual game appears in the narrative by John Young, Somerset Herald, of Princess Margaret's journey to Scotland when she was married to James IV.

On the night of 4 August 1503, her second at the castle of Dalkeith, not far from Edinburgh, the Princess was woken from her sleep by a great fire which had broken out in the stables. Lost in the fire were two white palfreys for which Margaret had a great affection. She was much distressed. Her leech no doubt prescribed a tincture of Golden Feverfew which Gerard says 'is good for such as be melancholic, sad, pensive and without speech'; but when the king called upon her the next day, in order to offer such comfort as he could, he found that she had a remedy of quite a different character. For on coming into the Princess's drawing-room he 'found her playing at cards . . .', and she, 'rising, advanced to meet him very gladly, of her goodwill kissing him. After that the king gave salute to all the ladies. He was dressed in a black velvet jacket, bordered with crimson velvet and edged with white fur.'

How sad it is that we hear no more of the cards used, or even how many players took a hand. Indeed no more is heard of the queen as a card player; though in the case of the king it is a different matter. The royal accounts show, among other items of a similar nature, a payment to 'Cuddy, the Inglis luter, to luse his cheyne of grotis, quhilk he lost at cards [to redeem his chain of groatis which he lost at cards]'; and William Dunbar, one of the greatest of Scots poets, makes several references to the king's card playing with the 'French Leich', otherwise John Damien. The latter was, no doubt, a dashing player since it was he who, according to Bishop Leslie, 'flew off the castle walls at Strivelling bot schortlie he fell to the ground and brak his thee [thigh] bane; not the wyt [blame] thereof he ascryvit to that thair was sum hen fedderis in the wings, quhilk yarnit [yearned for] and covet the mydding and not the skyis'.

It is in the clothes of this period that these court cards are dressed. Mr F. A. Repton, in an article 'on the costume of Coate-Cardes' in the *Gentleman's Magazine* for November 1843, writes: 'Many of the readers of the Gentleman's Magazine may not be aware that the dresses represented on our coate-cards are actually the same as those that prevailed about the time of Henry VII or VIII.' He then goes on to explain that the lappets on each side of the queen's faces, and the flat caps and striped stockings ('idiot-like, red, greene and yellows') complained of by the knave of hearts in Samuel Rowland's poem 'The Four Knaves' (1611) are from the period 1500–40. He adds that the queens' habit of wearing their crowns on the very backs of their heads continued until the end of the sixteenth century.

The accessories of the court cards are also of considerable interest even if of little help in dating the pack. The kings of spades and clubs are armed with a sword held upright before them in the manner of a modern officer on parade but with the difference that the kingly sword is held in the left hand. The king of hearts, also left-handed, holds his weapon of which only the hilt is visible, behind his head; he has neither the mien nor the stance of a man about to deliver a sweeping blow. The king of diamonds is alone in being armed with battle-axe. All the queens hold a flower in the left hand, while the queen of spades has in her right hand a sceptre which has been turned in the style of a period chair leg. The knave of clubs originally held an arrow, the point of which reached to the top of his head, and sported a feather in his cap, badges of office which in the passage of years have declined into an unimpressive staff and a small leaf: the knave of spades set out with a pike in his left hand, a weapon which has degenerated into a quite unrecognizable adjunct: the knave of hearts had, and has, a battleaxe in his left hand, and originally flourished a truncheon, or wand of office, in his right; but over the years the latter, by a series of mistakes by artists, has turned into a futile feather: and the knave of diamonds holds a staff with a hook a little way below the point which represents a little known weapon called a Welsh hook.

It is plain that before the fifteenth century was out the English were among the most devoted courtiers surrounding the cardboard royalty; to the extent, indeed, that their skill at archery, the very foundation of the country's military successes was imperilled by want of practice. Not surprisingly, Henry VIII tried, in 1526, to prohibit cards absolutely, together with dice and bowls, all of which were to be confiscated and burnt; but the prohibition was short lived as the young men 'fell to drinking, stealing, conies and other worse demeanours'. At the time he failed in his object; but fifteen years later a statute was passed which restricted the card playing of artificers, labourers and husbandmen, in addition to the service men and apprentices already restrained, to Christmastide. In the higher ranks of society, on the other hand, cards and dice were in such constant use, and, indeed, misuse, that they were considered seriously to reflect on the standards of contemporary life. Among the *Harleian Manuscripts* may be found an anonymous poem:

> Before thys tyme they lovyd for to juste
> And in Shootynge chefely they sett ther mynde,
> And their landys and possessions now sett they moste
> And at cardes and dyce ye may them fynde.

In the time of the next monarch, Elizabeth I, 'Dicers and carders because their abuses are as commonly cryed out on', says Stephen Gosse in *The Schoole of Abuse* (1579), 'as usually shown, have no needs of a neddelesse discourse, for every man seeth them, and they stinke almost in every man's nose.' With so much ill-feeling the card players were lucky not to be included among the 'Rogues, Vacabondes and Sturdye Beggars' of an Act of 1579 for whom the penalty was 'to bee grievously whipped'.

What were the games which so entranced the English people that they fluttered round the gaming table so devotedly? Charles Cotton, writing in the introduction to the *Compleat Gamester* (1674), says that Gleek and Angel-Beast were played in Tudor times; Joseph Strutt, writing almost exactly one hundred years later, claims Primero as the oldest known card game in England, adding that it was fashionable during the sixteenth century and was a game of which Queen Elizabeth was particularly fond. Alan Wykes, in *Gambling* (1964), 'catches glimpses of details of whist-like games in the sixteenth century. Triumph, ruff, ombre and honours', he says, 'were all built round the idea of trumping and are all developments of ronfa. . . .' *Ombre*, which became extremely popular in the middle of the seventeenth century, was once upon a time thought to have reached England with Catharine of Braganza, who married Charles II in 1662; but here the margin of error was greater even than in the case of tea which she was thought also to have brought to England. In the latter case the error was not less than forty-seven years: for tea, or *char* to be precise, is mentioned in a letter written by a Mr Wickham on 27 June 1615, and a tea house was opened in the City of London long before Catharine set foot on English shores. Piquet, a name derived from the French suit of *piques*, was also played in the sixteenth century. It was first known as Cent or Sant taken from its Spanish name of *Cientos* but changed its name after the marriage of Charles I to Henrietta Maria of France. It became more popular in the seventeenth century and has its adherents to this day.

Turning to the next century, Miss Elizabeth Burton in *The Jacobeans at Home* (1962) says:

> There were other games, besides whist, which continued popular.
> Primero, Gleek, English Ruff or Honours (often called Slam),
> French Ruff and One-and-Twenty. The latter developed
> variations under the names of Costly Colours and Bone-Ace.
> Rather dull games requiring small ingenuity were Plain Dealing,
> Queen Nazarine and Beast. All Fours was much favoured in
> Kent; and Post and Pair, which required considerable daring
> was, suitably enough, a West Country favourite. New to the
> century was cribbage, reputedly invented by the Cavalier poet
> Sir John Suckling, one of the greatest gallants of the time.

A story was put about that Sir John entered into an arrangement with those French card masters who exported their goods to England to mark their cards in a way known only to him; but since he poisoned himself because he had run through a vast fortune inherited from his father, and could not stomach the thought of poverty, it would seem that either he did not avail himself of his secret information or else the signs were never there in the first place. Other games were Maw, supposedly a weakness of James VI, and Lanterloo or Loo or Lue, Put, Brag, Quadrille, Quintille, Wit and Reason, Comet and Basset.

Basset was first played in London at the rooms of the Duchess Mazarin and quickly displaced *ombre* as the really fashionable game. But it was necessarily confined to the wealthy: for there was a possibility of tremendous losses. Nell Gwyn is said to have lost £5000 in a single night and the other royal mistresses, the Duchessess of Cleveland and Portsmouth lost even greater sums. The entry in the diary of John Evelyn for 4 February 1685, describing a visit to Whitehall, may be well known but cannot escape repetition in this connection.

> I can never forget the inexpressible luxury and prophaneness,
> gaming and all dissoluteness, and as it were total forgetfullnesse
> of God (it being Sunday evening) which this day se'nnight I was
> witnesse of, the King sitting and toying with his concubines,
> Portsmouth, Cleaveland, and Mazarine, &c. a French boy
> singing love songs, in that glorious gallery, whilst about 20 of the
> greate courtiers and other dissolute persons were at Basset round
> a large table, a bank of at least 2000 in gold before them upon

which two gentlemen who were with me made reflections of astonishment.

Sir Richard Steele (1672–1729), of *The Tatler*, *The Spectator* and *The Guardian* fame, took an excessively dim view of female gamblers. In *The Guardian* for 29 July 1713 he wrote:

Now there is nothing that wears out a fine face like the Vigils of the Card Table, and those cutting passions which naturally attend them. Hollow eyes, haggard looks, and pale Complexions, are the natural Indications of a Female Gamester. Her morning sleeps are not able to repair her Mid-night Watchings. I have known a woman carried off half dead from Bassette; and have many a time grieved to see a Person of Quality gliding by me, in her chair, at Two a Clock in the Morning, and looking like a Spectre amidst a Flare of Flambeaux. In short I never knew a thorough-paced female gamester hold her beauty two winters together.

That gambling was not confined to the upper classes is clear from the *Every Day Book* by William Home, in which it is reported that 'In October, 1735, a child of James and Elizabeth Leech, of Chester-le-Street in the county of Durham, was played for at cards, at the sign of the Salmon, one game, four shillings against the child, by Henry and John Trotter, Robert Thompson and Thomas Ellison, which was won by the latter and delivered to them accordingly.'

In order that he and his court might indulge in gaming in the greatest comfort and with the minimum of trouble, Charles II revived the appointment of the Groom-Porter, a member of the Lord Steward's department, who overlooked the furniture of the royal apartments and ensured that all was in order for the king's entertainments. He was, and had been since the time of Henry VIII, if not earlier, the official to whom all matters relating to gambling, whether cards or dice, had been entrusted. His authority seems to have been extended in 1706, for the *London Gazette* for December 6th to 10th of that year carried an announcement that the Groom-Porter of the day, Thomas Archer Esq., had:

full power to supervise, regulate, and authorise . . . all manner of gaming within this kingdom. And, whereas, several of Her Majesty's Subjects, keeping Plays or Games in their Houses have lately been abused, and had moneys extorted from them by several ill-disposed Persons contrary to the Law. These are, therefore, to give Notice, that no Person Whatsoever, not producing his Authority from the Groom-Porter, under Seal of his Office, hath any Power to Act anything under the said Patent . . .

And the notice goes on to say that all such abuses are to be notified to the Groom-Porter at his office 'at Mr Stephenson's, a Scrivener's House, over against Old Man's Coffee House, near Whitehall'. The Groom-Porter continued to preside over gaming until the reign of George III, who, madly disapproving of gambling, abolished the office.

The 'ill-disposed' persons who cheated the simple, unsophisticated English at cards were, in the general opinion, the French. Their reputation was so unsavoury that an attaché at the British Embassy in Paris, horrified at their sharp practices, took to warning his fellow countrymen against playing with people not well known to them. 'Even the ladies', he says, 'do not want tricks to strip a Bubble'.

Can the prosperity of a trade be gauged by the number of government appointed leeches, from which it suffers? The Groom-Porter, though without having any salary or specific fees attached to his post, undoubtedly prospered. Not for him the need to economize on snuff or roast swan or other delicacy or luxury of the age. Another such official was the Inspector of Playing Cards, who held a post of privilege, granted by the monarch, from which it was expected that the appointee would make a handsome profit. It could, therefore, be used as a reward for services rendered or in discharge of an inconvenient debt. In November 1615, Sir Richard Coningsby, in settlement of a debt of £1800 due from the crown surrendered his sole rights in the transportation of tin, undertook to pay King James an annual rent of £200, and in return was appointed to 'the office of viewing, searching and sealing all cards made in the kingdom, and to receive five shillings for every gross, as had been offered by the card makers, any cards proving false to be forfeited'. Exception was taken to this appointment by the haberdashers and other dealers in small wares. They made common cause with The Company of French Merchants in London, for whom there was no mitigation of the full amount of the charge which was on top of their liability to a customs duty of 2 shillings per gross of cards imported from France. The French claimed that Sir Richard's fee was an infringement of the terms of the Treaty between England and France and petitioned the High Court. The Court, founding its argument on the undoubted fact that the importation of cards from foreign parts was in any case totally prohibited by ancient law, held that the appointment of Sir Richard was illegal. He, however, also appealed and the matter came before the Privy Council. At that point the king intervened by instructing the Privy Council that the royal prerogative must be maintained, presumably a delicate way of saying that as His Majesty had no intention of paying Sir Richard the outstanding amount of £1800 that sum might well fall on right honourable shoulders were Sir Richard not appointed. Be that as it may, the appointment was confirmed and the French merchants allowed 'to take up such cards as they have brought out of France' the earlier laws not withstanding: after all, those cards were all grist to Sir Richard's mill. We can sympathize with Parliament's complaint that Sir Richard's fees were in fact 'an arbitrary and illegal' tax levied without the consent of Parliament.

From this case we can get some idea of the size of the trade. To obtain fees of £1 Sir Richard had to seal four gross, or 576, of packs. Before he could pay the king the annual rent of £200 he had to seal 115,200 packs. To do that, make good the loss of his income from the transportation of tin, which he had forfeited, and recover the £1800 in, say, five years, it would be necessary for him to seal something like half a million packs a year before he made any real profit. It is clear that not only were some of the English card masters in a big way of business, but, since the population of England has been estimated at 4,811,718 in the year 1600, some of them must have enjoyed as thriving and prosperous export trade as the alabaster carvers of Nottingham.

The bringing of playing cards into the country from foreign parts remained a thorny subject for a long time. When the Worshipful Company of Playing Card Manufacturers was founded by Royal Charter in 1628, the continued importation of playing cards into the realm is emphasized in the preamble and is given as the principal cause of financial distress among such of 'our loving subjects' as have 'used and put into practice the Art and Trade of making playing cards within our City of London'. And the first proviso is the complete prohibition, from 1 December 1628, of all importation of playing cards into England and Wales. No Customs Officer was to allow cards into the country upon payment of any composition, duty or subsidy whatsoever but must confiscate such cards which were to be declared forfeit. One would have thought that even if the earlier laws were ambiguous or in some other way difficult to interpret that such a clear embargo would have put an end to the matter; but to our astonishment we learn that twenty-three years later several poor card makers again complained that they were in danger of starving to death because of persistent infraction of the ancient laws and statutes. Yet again importation was absolutely prohibited by a committee appointed by Parliament for the Navy and Customs, and an order was given that the officers should seize all such cards, and proceed against the parties offending. Even that was not sufficient; for in 1684 there was a further petition and a further proclamation by the king, after which there are no further records of card masters petitioning their monarch to uphold the laws of the land. It may have been, of course, that they suffered the very fate which induced them to approach His Majesty in the first place and that they quietly starved to death. Or it may have been that they at last grasped that money was being made in high places by the handling of foreign cards and that, therefore, the ancient laws were unlikely to be strictly enforced and petitioning was a waste of time.

When founding the Worshipful Company the king saw to it that he would not lose by the arrangements. He was not content with the Worshipful Company's gift of a truly magnificent silk inlaid pack of cards and silver counters with the heads of all the English kings from William the Conqueror up to, and including, his own. He was at pains to point out that the revenue from customs duties and other impositions had up to the date of the Charter been considerable. He expected to be compensated; indeed, he insisted on it, and a clause was written into the Charter compelling the card masters to pay a duty of 2 shillings per gross and a further 1 shilling per gross to the officer appointed as Receiver of the Duty. The first Receiver was William Watkyns; and so that he and his successors should always be in a position to identify the manufacturer of any pack of cards each and every card master was required to use a 'print, stamp or mark of his own invention'. Many of the signs adopted were inn signs, and some of them we recognize to this day among the signs of public houses: The Crown, The Coach and Horses, and The Adam and Eve. After the Restoration there were Royalist signs such as General Monk's Head; but the most important, for they were to become marks of quality instead of identification, were King Henry VII entered in 1706, The Merry Andrew entered in 1714 and The Great Mogul, one of the marks of Philip Blanchard, an eminent card master who was Master of the Worshipful Company for the years 1724–5 and 1738–9, and the Valiant Highlander, both entered in 1741. In after years packs were known in the trade as Moguls, Harrys, Highlanders and Andrews according to quality and ranking in that order.

Great Mogul wrapper.
British Museum

In 1709 the Worshipful Company became agitated by a Bill introduced into Parliament: for its object was the 'Better Preventing' of excessive and immoderate gaming, an end that was to be achieved, so the Worshipful Company understood, by the total prohibition of cards, among other instruments of gambling, from all public houses. The Company foresaw destitution for their members and campaigned against the Bill. Its efforts were not unavailing: for though the Bill was accepted by Parliament, and became an Act, playing cards were not banned from public houses.

The Company was to have further experience of this sort of intrigue. The very next year, 1710, they energetically opposed the imposition of a tax of 6d per pack, part of the Government's plan to raise sufficient money to pay for Marlborough's campaigns in the Netherlands during the War of the Spanish Succession. Their opposition was unsuccessful, and the tax, contained in an Act for 'Licencing and Regulating hackney coaches and chairs . . . and for charging certain new duties . . . on cards and dice, and on the exportation of rock salt for Ireland', became effective from 11 June 1711. By this Act, no cards were to be removed from the card master's premises until the Commissioners appointed to receive the 'vellum Parchment and paper' duties had approved the seal upon the 'paper and thread enclosing every pack of cards'. The following year, another law provided, among other things, that one of the cards must be 'stamped or marked on the spotted or printed side'. Arising out of that provision the ace of spades became the card to be stamped on its face, and it has remained so ever since, being specifically mentioned in later legislation.

In December of 1712 the Master was compelled to sell a house in Spitalfields for the sum of £38 10s to help defray the costs of opposing the Government. Fryer, who was Master in 1648, falling ill, had 7 shillings collected for him by the wardens—who a little later contributed 40 shillings for the burial. It is as well that there were funds in hand, for the flow of legislation affecting playing cards was incessant for the next 150 years. In 1719 Parliament enacted a law imposing a fine of £10 on anyone found guilty of defrauding, or attempting to defraud, the Revenue by the use of old seals or stamps. In 1765 the card masters were required to send paper to the Commissioner and the latter were to have as many aces printed thereon as the former required: and it was also provided that of the two sixpenny stamps one should be on the ace of spades and one on the 'jew or wrapper', jew being a corruption of the French *jeu*, and it was further provided that there should be different aces of spades for the home and export markets. In 1776 the tax was raised to 1s 6d, and so that the aces should not become littered with stamps, the Commissioners were to obtain a new stamp for the full amount. In 1789 the duty was increased by yet another 6d and yet again the Commissioners were authorized to have a new stamp out; but no example has yet come to light.

In the next century, in the year 1800, an Act authorized a duty of 1s 5d a pack payable on all packs imported into Ireland. In 1801 the duty was raised by 6d per pack, making a total of 2s 6d. In 1804 an Act was passed by Parliament cancelling all duties, other than those imposed in the year 1801, on stamped vellum, parchment and paper and other articles on the expressed grounds that the duties 'are become very numerous, intricate and complicated' but leaving the tax at 2s 6d per pack. In 1815 an Act was passed concerning the stamps and seals on wrappers around cards made in Ireland, where production was restricted to the cities of Dublin, Cork and Limerick. In 1828 the tax was reduced to 1s per pack, not because the Government of the day was any less grasping but simply because the high rate was self-defeating and sales were falling seriously. It was this Act which provided that the duty must be 'denoted on the ace of spades of each pack', and this was the duty ace dubbed by the public 'Old Frizzle' because its curls and twirligigs reminded them of the perruquier's art. In 1862 the duty was reduced to 3d per pack and wrappers were to be destroyed on opening. Finally, in 1960 the duty was abolished all together.

The law relating to playing cards, the taxes imposed and the stamps indicating those taxes, are a study in themselves. They have been considered and analysed in detail by John Boynton Kaiser, whose monograph (with check lists by Samuel Marcus) entitled *British Playing Card Stamp Duties and their Authorized Stamps* was published by The American Philatelic Society in 1960.

Returning to the seventeenth century, the English card masters,

Astronomical cards. Stopforth & Son, *c.* 1828.
Collection Evelyn Goshawk; photo Peter Kibbles

NEPTUNE ♠

MERCURY ♥

MARS ♦

ARGO NAVIS ♣ ♣

MONOCEROS

ANTLIA PNEUMATICA

CANIS MAJOR

♣

♣ ♣

PISCIS VOLANS   CANOPUS

Decl 52°36'6'S. R.6°20'.1'

LYRA ♣

CYGNUS   DRACO

HERCULES

VULPECULA ET ANSER

♣

VEGA

Decl.38°37'22'N. R.18°30'''

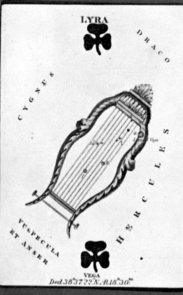

CENTAURUS ◆ ◆

HYDRA CONTINUAT

LEPUS

CRUX

ROBUR CAROLI

◆ ◆

ALPHA

Decl.60°6'33'S. R.14°28'''

CYGNUS ▲

VULPECULA ET ANSER

LYRA

LACERTA

CEPHEUS

▲

DENEB

Decl.44°36'32'N. R.20°35'

CAMELOPARDALIS ♥

URSA MINOR

DRACO   TARANDUS

CUSTOS MESSIUM

URSA MAJOR

LYNX

AURIGA   PERSEUS

♥

CANIS MAJOR ◆

MONOCEROS

LEPUS

ARGO NAVIS

COLUMBA NOACHI

◆

SIRIUS

Decl.16°28'11'S. R.6°37'''

The Gaming Plate by John
Bickam, London 1741.
'The Universal Penman; or,
The Art of Writing made
useful to the Gentleman and
Scholar, as well as the Man of
Business.'
Collection Weinreb and
Douwma Limited, London

face p. 64

GAMING.

The Diversion of Cards and Dice,
however Engaging, are oftner Provocatives
to Avarice and Loss of Temper, than mere
Recreations and innocent Amusements.

Here Scaramouch and Harlequin, at Gaming can't agree;
They Quarrel, and poor Scaramouch is tumbl'd down you see.

All Cheats at Cards, still gaping for their prey,
Quarrels create; and Mischiefs follow Play:
It loses Time, disturbs y Mind and Sense,
Whilst Oaths and Lies are oft the consequence,
And Murders, sometimes, follow loss of Pence.

John Bickham Scrip:

Opposite
Court cards from a pack made
by Hall and Son for George III.
Collection Evelyn Goshawk;
photo Peter Kibbles

114

Geographical cards, *c.* 1827.
The King of Spades is said to
represent George Washington.
British Museum

ELECTION NEWS.

Cards from an American
transformation pack, *c.* 1900.
Slide collection Roger Tilley

Four court cards and four aces from a pack by Ludlow and Co., England, late eighteenth century. The aces represent the four Orders of chivalry: spades the Order of the Garter 1344, diamonds the Order of the Bath 1499, clubs the Order of the Thistle 1703, and hearts the Order of St Patrick 1783. Collection Evelyn Goshawk; photo Peter Kibbles

who till then had followed the patterns set by their continental counterparts by printing cards for educational purposes as well as cards for playing games, now started a new fashion by producing cards which satirized contemporary affairs, made political and religious propaganda, and illustrated current events. Is it not curious that the card masters appear to have anticipated the great age of literary satire? Of the notable satirists only Dryden, whose 'Absolom and Achitophel' was published in 1681, can be said to be contemporaneous with the age of cardboard ridicule.

At first glance the first of this new series of cards scarcely qualifies under any of the above headings. Known as *The Spanish Armada* pack and published about 1680, the cards illustrate the defeat of the Armada nearly one hundred years earlier; but that it was intended as anti-Catholic propaganda, possibly as a protest against the Catholic leanings of James II, is shown by the inclusion of Armada scenes in a later pack called *All the Popish Plots*. Seventeenth-century English protest or not, the sixteenth-century Spaniards, it may be guessed, protested loudly and frequently against the 'orders set down . . . to be observed in the Voyage towards England' by their commander the Duke of Medina: for His Excellency ordered not only that the soldiers were to have their rooms clean and unpestered with chests 'but that neither soldiers nor sailors nor mariners were to be allowed cards', and if by any chance they were to be discovered to be in possession of a pack, that pack was immediately to be confiscated and the Duke 'advertised'.

One of the first truly satirical packs was published about 1680. Announced as *A complete political Satire of the Commonwealth* it sets out to denigrate Cromwell and his colleagues. The ten of clubs, for example, shows the Lord Protector and four of his entourage kneeling in prayer, while through an embrasure the public executioner, axe held high, can be seen on the point of decapitating the king. Below the picture is the sentence 'Oliver seeking God while the king is murthered by his order'; and above it is a horizontal panel showing the suit sign in its left-hand corner and the number of the card—X—in the right. This arrangement of panel, picture and sentences became the standard format for this type of card. Among other Parliamentarian leaders decried, some more villanously than others, are Sir Arthur Hazelrigg, who appears on the eight of diamonds as 'Don Hazelrigg, knight of the Coddled Braine'; Sir H. Mildmay who, on the king of diamonds, 'solicits a citizen's wife for which his own corrects him'; and Major General Lambert, who is described on the eight of hearts, where he is shown standing in his garden with a large tulip in his hand, as The Knight of the Golden Tulip. Deprived of his commands by Cromwell and banished to Guernsey by the king, General Lambert spent his time cultivating and drawing flowers, in which he had long been intensely interested. Unless there is some seventeenth-century *double entendre* about the word tulip it is difficult to see any serious defamation in this card.

Returning to the anti-Catholic theme, we have *The Horrid Popish Plot*; *All the Popish Plots* with twenty-seven cards referring to the Spanish Armada, fourteen to The Gunpowder Plot, three to Dr Parry's Plot and eight to Titus Oates' Plot; *The Meal Tub Plot*, in which Thomas Dangerfield, in turn soldier, coiner, thief and perjurer, hatched a plot, or pseudo plot, against the Roman Catholic Duke of York; *The Rye House Plot* to rid the country at one and the same time of Charles II, held to be a secret Catholic, and the Duke of York, an avowed Catholic; *The Reign of James II* depicting events leading up to the Revolution of 1688; and *The Duke of Monmouth's Rebellion*, which was a plot to put the Protestant Duke upon the Throne of England. Of these packs *The Horrid Popish Plot* proved to be the most popular and was published in at least two editions, one of which was highly coloured and had court cards with medallion portraits, the kings and queens being royalty and the knaves the Pope in his beeskip headdress in all four suits. In all of these packs, issued in the decade 1678–88 there is plenty of 'blood and thunder', with the plotters strangling their victims and

Over the page
Modern playing cards: *Alchemists* by Müller, Switzerland (top left); *Jacob's Bible* cards, Israel (middle left); *Romance Espagnol* by Fournier, Spain (bottom left); *Can-Can* by Philibert, Paris (top right); *Cashmere* by Piatnik, Austria (middle right); *World Bridge* by Modiano, Italy (bottom right).
Collection Evelyn Goshawk; photo Peter Kibbles

KÖNIG

OBER

UNDER

K — K
DAVID
LIL

Q — Q
QUEEN OF SHEBA
ACCURATE

J — J
JOAB

K

Q

K

V ♣ 6

Hanging Proteſtants in ye West.

VI ♣ 7

I'le huff ye Dr Huff for all your huff:

Two Bⁿˢ: and Iudge Ienner Speake rudely to Dr Huff

VIII ♣ 9

The Tryal of the Seaven Bishops.

IX ♣ 10

The Seaven Biſhops going to the Tower.

themselves being hanged, drawn and quartered, with throat-cutting and all manner of gruesome details.

In a group of historical packs may be found *The Impeachment of Dr Sacheverell*, *The Events of the Reign of Queen Anne* and *Marlborough's Victories*. Dr Sacheverell attacked the principles of the Revolution Settlement both from the pulpit of St Paul's and at the Derby Assizes. He was impeached for high treason, found guilty, lightly sentenced and, being puffed up at his prominence on a pack of cards, spent the rest of his life quarrelling with his parishioners who failed, as he thought, to appreciate his importance. In this pack, illustrating the affair from the point of view of his supporters, miniature cards are used to indicate value instead of Roman numerals. *The Reign of Queen Anne* (engraved by R. Spofforth) illustrates military victories such as the 'Taking of Gibralter by Sir George Rook 24 July 1704', and more general subjects such as 'The Dreadful Storme November 26 1703', 'Her Majesty touching for Evil' and so forth. A feature of this pack is a small Arabic number, just above the centre of the lower line of the horizontal panel, marking the sequence of events. *Marlborough's Victories* seems to be a second instalment of *The Reign of Queen Anne*: far from being confined to his victories it has much to say on other matters, and a better title would be 'Marlborough and his times'. The three of spades shows 'The Duke of Anjou whipping Cardinal Porto-carero for forging a will of the late King of Spain'; while the seven shows Louis XIV on his throne examining the contents of a treasure chest with caption beneath which runs: 'Thus all my Spongey Officers I serve/Squeeze out their ill got wealth and let 'em starve.' In this pack there is no horizontal panel at the top of the cards, and the suit signs and value figures have changed sides.

The taste for satire spread overseas, and in 1719 a Dutch anti-Catholic pack was put on the market that was as vicious as any published. That Rome resented the cards was demonstrated by their prescription so that no good Catholic could use them without having to confess and do penance. Wherever possible these cards were to be burnt.

In England, 1770–71 saw the production of the so-called Bubble packs. *All the Bubbles* warns the players against investing in any of the spurious ventures cried about town. The promoters of these schemes 'cried they out like vultures', as Ben Jonson says, and urged upon the public every sort and kind of get-rich-quick speculation by which many an innocent was bled freely of his money. *The South Sea Bubble* pack is confined to the single, named scheme which, in the first place, was advanced by Lord Treasurer Harley in an effort to liquidate the floating debt arising out of the War of Spanish Succession. The public, unintentionally misled by Government support of the South Sea Company and intentionally misled by the unscrupulous directors, continued to invest blindly even after the outbreak of war with Spain put an end to all hope of sharing in the treasures of the South Seas.

Trial of the Seven Bishops. Led by Sancroft, Archbishop of Canterbury, the seven bishops who refused to obey James II's order to read the Declaration of Indulgence in 1688, were tried at the Tower of London and aquitted on June 30th. This was a death-blow to the rule of James II who fled the country when William of Orange landed in England in November 1688.
Bodleian Library, Oxford

Russian *trappola* cards.
British Museum

French costume pack, hand-
coloured engravings by
Migeon, Paris 1860.
Collection Evelyn Goshawk;
photo Peter Kibbles

The pack was marketed by Carington Bowles of St Paul's Churchyard, a map and print seller and a book publisher whose list included the works of the far from sprightly historical and antiquarian writer William Coxe.

Once again Holland followed suit and produced two Bubble packs, each satirizing the disastrous Mississippi scheme projected in France by John Law of Lauriston. Comparing the two packs, there was little

Eighteenth-century love cards.
Bodleian Library, Oxford

He plyes the Lady close with love and wit
But money only gains the wanton Titt.

So to the rough alarm, of war retreat.
While you the Sister Loves in combat meet.

O Lytherea, take the fatall Choice.
or Veil your beauty or Suppress your voice.

The verdant Spring nature her Self conspires.
To crown with endles Joys, Our Soft desires.

Corelli need not play to charm this fair
Much courser musick Suits her rurall ear.

When hearts are stake at if odd game call'd Love.
Is hard to guess, which does the looser prove.

A certain Gold-Smith, when the Stocks run high, —
Set up his Coach his Pride to gratify ;
But South Sea falling, left his Coach at 'Change,
And Shipping took, the distant World to Range .

A Lady Pawns her Jewels by her Maid ,
And in declining Stock, presumes to Trade ,
Till in South Sea at length she Drowns her Coin ,
And now in Bristol Stones, is glad to shine .

difference in the pictures, some difference in the captions and complete difference in the titles. The first pack was called *Kaart Spel van Momus Naar de Nieuwste Mode* and the second *Pasquin's Windkaart op de Windbegoti van 't Isar 1720*.

The eighteenth century also saw the production of packs devoted to a host of different, unconnected subjects. In the year 1700, or thereabouts, *Love Mottoes* on 'The Intrigues and Amusements of that Passion merrily displayed' became available to the purchaser. The cards have miniature cards in the top right-hand corner, a romantic picture in the middle and at the bottom a couple of lines which sometimes give good advice. Thus two young women on the king of clubs are warned: 'Yee Beautious Pair, forsake this gloomy way/Forbidden Love your Innocence may betray.' First *Proverbs* and then *Anecdotes* and *Aphorisms*, sometimes called *Witty Sayings*, followed about ten years later. Both had much the same format as *Love Mottoes*, except that *Proverbs* omitted the miniature card and *Aphorisms* had a general title on the upper right hand side to balance the miniature card on the left. The *Aphorisms*, of which there were anything up to nine on a card as opposed to a single *Anecdote*, were prosy rather than witty, practical rather than humorous. On the queen of hearts, under the general

title of 'Housewifery and Family Government', is to be found: 'A Sceptre is one thing a Ladle another.' A second series of *Proverbs* appeared about ten years later.

Soon after Gay's extremely successful *Beggar's Opera* was produced in 1727, Carington Bowles was offering for sale playing cards with the usual miniature card in the top left-hand corner but with the tune and verse from one of the lyrics in the body and the title of the song and the name of the singer at the top: the two of spades, for example, is headed by the sentence 'Tune of Twas when the Sea was roaring etc. sung by Lucy Lockit'. Carington also published William Coxe's *Life of John Gay*, and there is no surprise in learning that at the time of the death of his father, John Bowles, in 1779, with whom he had been in partnership, Carington was 'possessed of a plentiful fortune'. Another example of a musical pack is one brought out about 1780 by Longman and Lucy. Entitled *Complete Pack of new Cotillons adapted for the Harpsichord, Violin, G. Flute etc., with Figures entirely new*, the layout was very similar to that of its predecessor.

Other packs in the 'fun' category were *Aesop's Fables* printed by I. Kirk who was a neighbour and competitor of Carington Bowles in St Paul's Churchyard. The same style holds good, with the miniature card in one corner, a title at the top, and a picture illustrating the fable underneath. *London Cries* appeared in 1797, *Vices and Virtues* at much the same time, and *Fortune Telling* at the turn of the century. About 1780 a pack which is well known despite the fact that it never achieved popularity was put out by Rowley & Co. In an effort to get the card player away from the traditional suit signs and figures, Rowley & Co. chose shamrocks, chalices, pikeheads and cut diamonds of a design peculiar to the pack and printed in red, green, blue and yellow respectively. The kings and queens have been given over to European royalty and the knaves to soldiers.

A combination of 'fun' and education is to be found in an alphabetical pack by T. Foubert in 1757, in which all four knaves show the great actor David Garrick in one of his many roles, and a natural history pack with a drawing of a bird or beast on each card beneath its printed name. Full-blooded educational packs were another alphabetical pack published at the beginning of the century which announces: 'These cards was truly well designed/To ground all letters in youth's minde', lines which may not have inspired in parents that confidence in the compiler for which he hoped; a hand-coloured Biblical pack, put out about 1790; *The Elements of Astronomy and Geography explained in forty cards, beautifully engraved and coloured by the Abbé Paris published by J. Wallis of Ludgate St in 1795*: and *The Geography of England and Wales accurately delineated on 52 cards, including boundaries, extent, products, manufactures, etc., of each county* also published by J. Wallis, but in 1799.

An interesting though incidental use for cards was found in their backs, which were normally plain white, sometimes blue. They made

Left
Court cards from the *Four Corners of the World*, Dondorf 1886.
Collection Evelyn Goshawk; photo Peter Kibbles
See also page 163

Copy of a Titian self-portrait painted on the back of an eighteenth-century German card.

NED CRUSTY.

I won't, and I will;
And I don't, and I do;
I will have my own way;
Well, and what's that to you?

BILLY OVERALL.

Here's the tippy, here's the go:
Bucks and bloods all wear them fo.

CAPTAIN SWAGGER.

Here! hilloa! hark ye! hip! I fay,
Stand by you dog, and clear the way.

Mʳˢ Midnight

*This matron like the nightingale,
Tells to the Moon her Amorous tale.*

MASTER NINNY.

I'm fuch a ninnyhammer,
I don't know a word of my grammar.

BILLINGSGATE NELL.

I am bawling and fqualling from
morning till night,
And a fine game of romps is my
daily delight.

MISS PLATTERFACE.

On the charms of my face
You cannot fay wrong;
For fay what you will,
'Tis as broad as 'tis long.

MRS. DANDLE PUPPY.

Whene'er I walk with John or Joey,
Under my arm rides little Chloe.

Late-eighteenth-century
English cards.
Bowes Museum, Durham

most excellent memorandum pads. John Gay, for instance, wrote a couplet of the *Beggar's Opera* on the back of a nine of clubs: and the Reverend Augustus Toplady is often said to have written that favourite hymn, Rock of Ages, on the back of a six of diamonds, though there appears to be no supporting evidence. The owner of an *unter* of acorns with a portrait of a bearded man in mediaeval robes on the back thinks it possible that the picture is a self-portrait of Titian. But the commonest use of the backs was by callers at private houses who, finding that the person they wished to see was away from home, wanted to leave a

130

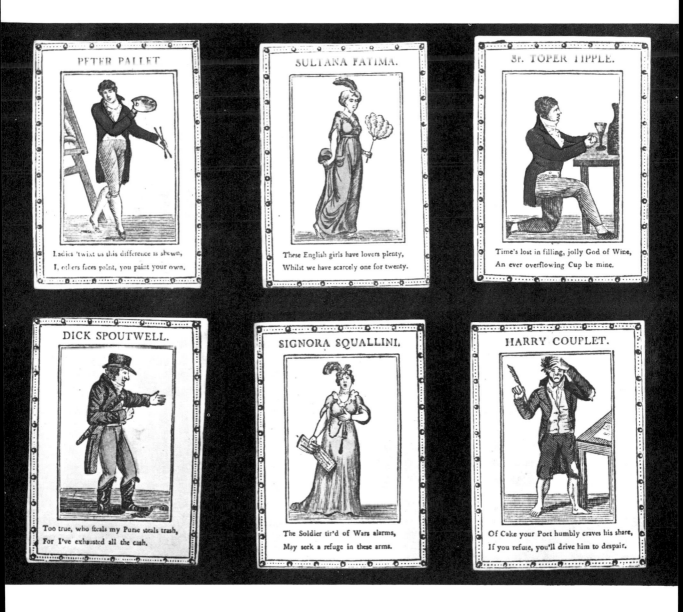

PETER PALLET

Ladies 'twixt us this difference is shewn,
I, others faces paint, you paint your own.

SULTANA FATIMA.

These English girls have lovers plenty,
Whilst we have scarcely one for twenty.

Sr. TOPER TIPPLE.

Time's lost in filling, jolly God of Wine,
An ever overflowing Cup be mine.

DICK SPOUTWELL.

Too true, who steals my Purse steals trash,
For I've exhausted all the cash.

SIGNORA SQUALLINI.

The Soldier tir'd of Wars alarms,
May seek a refuge in these arms.

HARRY COUPLET.

Of Cake your Poet humbly craves his share,
If you refuse, you'll drive him to despair.

Volunteers, c. 1840. English card
game.
Bowes Museum, Durham

message. For this purpose they were handed a pack of cards on the back of one or two of which they wrote whatever it was they wished to say. From this custom developed the visiting card, which at first was no more than a quarter of a back of a playing card on which the caller wrote his name.

Use of the backs was not entirely new. In Elizabethan times miniatures, other than those in oil, were painted on the thinnest possible vellum, made from the skin of an unborn lamb and carefully prepared. Basil S. Long says, in *British Miniaturists,* that the great Nicholas

131

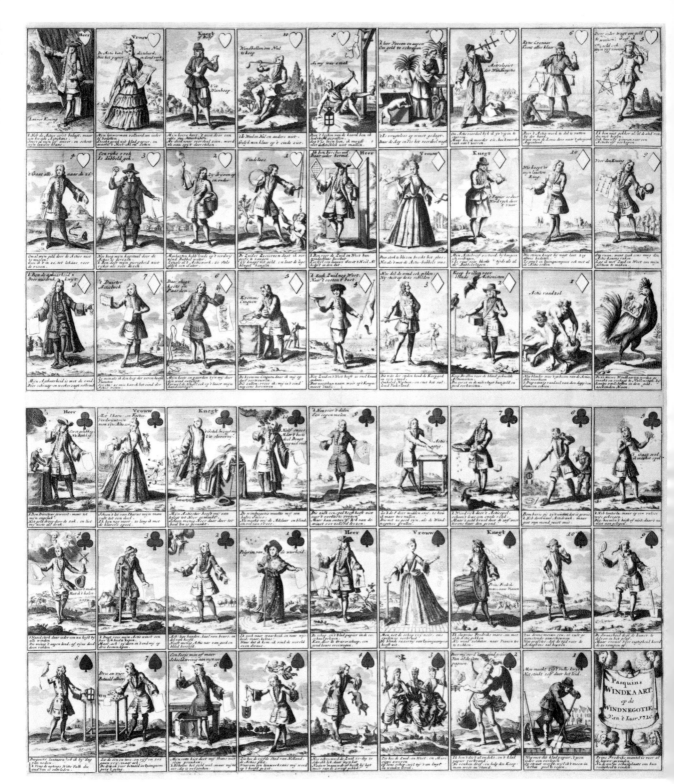

Hilliard's recipe for preparing the base or 'tablet', runs 'know also that parchment is the only good and best thing to limn on, but it must be virgin parchment such as never bore hair. It must be finely dressed, as smooth as any satin, and pasted with starch, well stretched on pasteboard, well burnished that it may be pure, without specks or stains, very smooth and white.' The necessary pasteboard was provided by playing cards since at that time it was for them, and for them only, that the material was manufactured. When, about the year 1700, thin, transparent ivory plates, with gold or silver or copper plate backing, began to be used that, too, was stuck to playing cards. The purpose in the first case was to prevent cockling and in the second to stop cracking. George C. Williams, joint author with Percy Buckman of *The Art of Miniature painting*, notes 'on two miniatures, quite evidently by Holbein, the pigments have been laid direct on the card without the intervention of the fine piece of parchment, and probably if there is one case there are others similar.' The latter statement is almost certainly true since, if nothing else, there were bound to be experiments.

A miniature of Mary Queen of Scots on just such a 'tablet' as described by Nicolas Hilliard is in the Royal Collection at Windsor Castle. Van der Doorst, Keeper of the King's Pictures to Charles I, records:

> Done upon the right light, the second picture of Mary Queen of Scotland upon a blew-grounded square card, dressed in her hair, in a carnation habit laced with small, gold lace and a string of pearls about her neck, in a little plain falling band she putting upon her second finger her wedding ring. Supposed to have been done by the said Jennet. Length three inches, breadth two inches.

Jennet is said by J. J. Foster, in *Chats on Old Miniatures*, to have been a misspelling of Janet, who in fact, was none other than the 'well-known Janet otherwise called François Clouet, Court Painter in France at the time of Queen Mary's betrothal to the Dauphin'.

It was towards the end of the eighteenth century that, as a result of an artist's mistake, the king of clubs' hand disappeared with the result that his orb, to all appearances, became an early English sputnik floating through space.

Pasquin's *Windkaart* ('Het Groote Tafereel der Dwaasheid', Amsterdam 1720). Published in *This Great Theatre of Folly*, a collection of broadsides and satirical prints relating to John Law and the Mississippi swindle. Collection Weinreb and Douwma Limited, London

133

Nothing better illustrates the fascination of playing cards and gaming than their earliest history in New England: for not even the almost total denial by the austerities of pioneer life of opportunities for recreation, as the result of the harsh and narrow spirit of Puritanism, could entirely prevent the colonists from yielding to the attraction of the 'Devil's Picture Books'. In this matter the Pilgrim Fathers, (who only acquired that proud title at the bicentennial celebration of their landing at Plymouth, having previously been referred to at first as Old Comers, and later as Forefathers), were no more able than other folk to erect a dyke high enough or strong enough to keep out the tides of temptation when at the spring. Even Virginia, where consciences were much less tender, found it necessary, as early as 1624, to promulgate a law bidding the very 'Mynisters' not 'to spend their time idelie' and forbidding them to play cards: while in 1633 certainly, if not before, the citizens of Plymouth Colony, the bed-rock of Puritanism in America, were fined for just that soul-destroying indulgence.

Neither the games played nor the cards used by the religious renegades have been recorded; but it can be taken for granted that the cards were of English origin shipped out from the mother country along with other goods, and, like as not, packed cheek by jowl with Bibles and prayer books. For domestic production had not been established, and good taste preferred English cards to French or Dutch.

English cards persisted. For the next hundred and fifty years or so advertisements appeared offering cards for sale but though it is possible that some were produced locally none of the advertisers claimed that that was the case. It was not until after the Declaration of Independence, and the Stamp Act, which placed a tax of one shilling upon every pack of cards 'sold or used within the said colonies or planatations', that, so far as we know, cards were printed in America. Even then they were printed from wood blocks imported from England. Perhaps the earliest known record of domestic manufacture is an advertisement in the *Federal Gazette* of 19 February, 1790, offering 'Ryves and Ashmead's Super-fine American manufactured Playing Cards . . .' which was unearthed by Catharine Perry Hargrave, who tells us, that Jazaniah Ford 'is the first American to be designated as card-maker'. He was born in 1757. Ryves and Ashmead apart, there were Amos Whitney, born in 1766 who towards the end of 1799 was offering for sale 'Super-fine Columbian, Harry the Eighth and Merry Andrew Playing Cards' at his manufactory (in the American trade 'Columbian' replaced 'Mogul' as the designation of the highest quality) ; James Y. Humphries who offered cards of both English and American manufacture in December 1800; and Thomas Crehore, who was born in 1769 and was called card-maker in a deed of 1801. These and other manufacturers must have had an uphill task for some time, partly because it was only in the first quarter of the nineteenth century that changing public attitudes towards recreation made card playing on any scale at all possible, and partly because of the continuing taste, by no means confined to America, for cards of a familiar design. Americans, however much they may have been irked by the Stamp Act even though it was promptly repealed, so much preferred English cards that up to the reign of William IV, it was quite a common practice to add 'London' to an ace that had never crossed the Atlantic and even to publish packs under a fictitious English name.

Even if Jazaniah Ford were not the first American card master a pack manufactured by him and dated by Catherine Perry Hargrave 'c.1800' appears to be the first to have distinctively designed court cards. Another characteristic of these cards is the decoration of the robes of the kings of clubs with the letter f.

In the field of cards and card-making the 'commemorative syndrome' appears to have been started by Jazaniah Ford. His *Decatur* pack, printed in 1814 to commemorate the American naval commander's capture of a British frigate during the Anglo-American war, had a sea battle scene on the upper part of the ace of spades; and some of the courts were dressed in Turkish clothes in remembrance of Decatur's feat of arms in Tripoli harbour. The pack was re-issued in 1824 to mark the visit of General Lafayette to the States, and for this purpose the ace of Spades was re-designed, the sea fight being omitted and a medallion portrait of Lafayette included in the middle of the sketch. From then onwards special packs of playing cards have been printed in many different countries to commemorate all kinds of events.

Legend has it that Abel Bowen (1790–1850) engraved the Lafayette pack; but who engraved Jazaniah Ford's first cards? Dr Alexander Anderson, who was born in 1775, is generally accepted as the first engraver on wood in America. He is known to have engraved wrappers for playing cards, is suspected of graving one for the Decatur packs, and though he is not known to have created any cards he seems a likely choice. The point cannot, however, be proved and must remain a matter of surmise. Other engravers of the period who may have worked on cards, though no-one can say for certain, that such was the case, were Samuel Hill, who was in active business from about 1785 onwards; John Bowen, working in Philadelphia roughly from 1810 to 1820; the famous American patriot and hero of Longfellow's 'Midnight Ride of Paul Revere'; and Joseph Alexander Adams who was born in 1803 and most of whose work before he was established was, according to W. J. Linton in *The History of Wood Engraving in America*, 'for labels for cotton goods, or soap stamps, hand bills, playing cards and such like'.

J. V. Humphries asserted his individuality as a card master by printing, round about the turn of the century, a pack in which the kings are Presidents—Washington, Adams, Jefferson and Jackson—the queens Goddesses—Venus, Justice, Ceres and Athena—and the knaves Red Indians—three of whom were recognized (no names are given on the cards) as Joseph Brant, Red Jacket and Gy-and-Wachia, the fourth unidentified. The first two knaves were exceptional men deserving their places in the pack. Both were hereditary chieftains, Brant of the Mohawks and Red Jacket of the Senecas; both supported the British forces during the Revolution; the first was a missionary of the Anglican Church and taught religion to the Mohawks, the latter strongly opposed the introduction of Christianity to his people; and Joseph Brant finally led the Six Nations, which included the Senecas as well as his own tribe, into the reservation prepared for them on the Grand River in Ontario.

J. Y. Humphries also manufactured forty-eight card packs with Spanish symbols, presumably for export to Mexico and for use by some of the Indian tribes. From the very beginning American card masters exported a proportion of their output, partly, no doubt, because of the home consumer's insistence on English goods. As early as 1792 Massachusetts exported 1000 packs, while in the preceding year over 19,000 packs were imported. By 1814 the annual production of the United States had reached a total of 400,000 packs, and their card makers were obviously beginning to hold an extablished place in the market.

The Americans not only used English, or English type cards; they played the games their ancestors had brought from England or which they themselves brought back after a visit to the homeland. Loo and post-and-pair seem to have been particularly popular (Jefferson is said to have played the latter in the intervals of composing the Declaration of Independence), then whisk, and later faro. The popularity rating of the last received a considerable boost after the purchase, in 1803, of Louisiana, where the game had been taken by the French when they settled the province in 1699. Frances Trollope, mother of Anthony Trollope, in *Domestic Manners of the Americans*, first published in 1832, says 'Their large evening parties are surprisingly dull: the men sometimes play cards by themselves, but if a lady plays it must not be for money; no écarté, no chess. . . .' That experience was in Maryland. Elsewhere in the book, speaking of the Cincinnatians, she says 'Billiards are forbidden, so are cards. To sell a pack of cards in Ohio subjects the seller to a penalty of fifty dollars.' There was an American version of whist, known as Whist Bostonien or, more generally, Boston. Invented by French Officers serving in America during the War of Independence, this game took the reverse route of the others, being taken, later, to England from the States by some Russian officers who had been visiting America. Another version of whist played in Russia at much the same time, in which trumps ceased to be a matter of chance, was

Union playing cards, New York 1862. Suits are American flags, stars, shields and eagles. Queens are goddesses of liberty, kings are infantry officers and jacks are artillery officers. Bodleian Library, Oxford

136

American transformation cards
advertising Murphy Varnish,
nineteenth century.
Bodleian Library, Oxford
(see page 146)

carried by Russian officers into Turkey, whence it spread westwards,
eventually reaching the United States of America and finally nearly
every corner of the world. In Russia the game was called Biritsch, a
word that in the course of its travels from Near East to Far West
became corrupted into Bridge.

Cards and card designs were not the only way in which Americans
copied their English relatives. They saw the advantages of educational
packs, and from the end of the eighteenth century, that is to say more
or less as soon as they began to print their own cards, they turned out a
fairly steady stream. *Various Employments* appeared in Pennsylvania
towards the end of the eighteenth century, the pack being of the
customary design in that each card is largely given over to an illustration, in this case, of a skilled craft, with room at the foot for two or three
lines of text. There are no indices. Geographical, geometrical, grammatical and alphabetical cards were offered for sale in Boston in 1811;
from 1843 onwards *Scripture History*, *Authors* and a variety of other
games were printed at Salem, after Plymouth the oldest city in New

American transformation
cards, c. 1800.
Bodleian Library, Oxford
see also page 117

138

England. In 1845 *Shakespeare, a Card Game,* and *The Game of Kings* were published in New York; and in Philadelphia, also in 1845, well-intentioned mothers and fathers could buy '*The New Impenetrable Secret, or young lady's and gentleman's Polite Puzzle, being an entirely new set of entertaining cards. . . . The whole designed, while they amuse and entertain, to establish principles of virtue and modesty in the minds of both sexes.*' The Americans also adopted the English habit of cutting up playing cards to make visiting cards, used the backs for invitations to parties, as memo pads and for drawing silhouettes.

Further north, an additional, quite novel use was found for card backs. This was the introduction into French Canada, in 1685, of card money at a time when the Intendant of Justice, Police and Finance, the Seigneur Jacques de Nuelles, was faced with a shortage of coin. Having exhausted all the sources from which he could borrow funds with which to pay the troops, he resorted to the use of cards (first calling in all packs) either whole or cut into halves or quarters, thereby getting three values. These pieces of cardboard, endorsed with their value and signed by the Governor and the Intendant, were redeemable in supplies when the latter reached Canada from France. In 1714 there was no less than 1,600,000 francs of this most original and useful currency in circulation. Indeed it proved so successful that though originally intended as a temporary measure to be used once, and once only, it was re-introduced at varying intervals up to 1763.

If we are to believe Sir William Maxwell Stirling, the nineteenth century opened most inauspiciously for the arts in Spain. In *Annals of the Artists of Spain* Sir William damns, if not outright at least with only slight relief, Spanish culture of the period. Writing of Charles IV, he says 'No enlightened patronage of art or letters could be expected from the drivelling tool of Godoy. . . . But he and his family, the most despicable of the royal houses which disgraced Europe at the close of the century, were at least happy in a portrait painter, Francisco Goya, an artist worthy of a better time.' That Godoy was able, in public, and without reproof, to describe the queen, Maria Louisa the Unchaste, to the king himself as 'a rich old lady whose name I have forgotten' goes far to support Sir William's views. Whatever the case generally, it was far from being an unhappy one for this particular branch of the Graphic arts, since several lovely packs were printed about this time. One, which according to the legend on the ace of coins was '*Grabada en Madrid por D. Jose Martinez de Castro Ano de 1810*, not only had the court cards beautifully and imaginatively drawn but also had the fours decorated in the middle with enchanting little scenes. All the cards

Spanish cards, *c.* 1810.
Collection Roger Tilley

were splendidly coloured. In another pack of this period the court cards were dressed in contemporary military dress and again the fours were decorated with small vignettes, one being a Peruvian worshipping the rising sun and another Bacchus dancing before a statue. Solesia y Cia, Don Pedro Castillo, F. Ocejo and the Royal Manufactory all of Madrid, and Torras & San Martino and Sarbat 7 Sole Barna of Barcelona, were among those who turned out good work at this period. The well known French firm of Jean Volay of Thiers was also active in the Spanish market; but its work was not up to the standard of the others.

At the very beginning of the century, indeed possibly in the last year or two of the preceding century, the Spaniards introduced a number of breaks into the border line of their cards, three breaks indicating the suit of *bastos*, two that of *espadas* and one that of *copas*. The suit of *oros* was given a continuous line. While it is difficult to see the object of this arrangement, since it still leaves the player with the necessity of looking at the suit signs to ascertain the value of any card, it is still in use today and presumably will continue to be used. At much the same time Spanish card masters started numbering their cards, the figure appearing in the top-left corner and the bottom right; but since this practice was far from becoming general until the last quarter of the century, it cannot be argued that together with the broken line they enabled a player to tell the value of each of his cards without spreading out his hand and thus making it easier for an

Spanish cards. Suits are *espadas* and *bastos*.

opponent to see what cards he held. It is a pity that generally speaking, the bottom right-hand figures are engraved so as to appear upside down and back to front.

Travelling north from Spain, we pass into France where we are confronted by two packs with but a single aim and neither very successful. The first of the two, which appeared in 1810, was designed by Jacques Louis David, the painter who was a Deputy during the Convention who, artistically speaking, dominated the revolutionary and imperial period, and whom Napoleon appointed as his 'first painter' in 1804. Among David's commissions was one to design a pack

French pack designed by Jacques Louis David 1810. Bodleian Library, Oxford intended by Napoleon to replace the regional designs and become the standard pack of France. In this sequence the Emperor, in the costume of Julius Caesar and with a crown of laurel leaves, appeared as the king of diamonds. In the following year a pack by Gatteaux, 'graveur des medailles au Roi', was put on the market. It, too, had court cards in the form of Biblical or classical figures (Hildegard, Abigail, David and Alexander), though they were less well drawn than those of David. Neither pack appealed to the French public and in 1813 the old-fashioned, pre-Revolution figures of the Paris design once more came into their own, though only after they had been changed somewhat by Gatteaux.

Still travelling north, though bearing to the east, we reach Germany and find an entirely novel and most important innovation. In 1805 the great German publishing house of Cotta, established at Tübingen in

Dame

Jeanne d'Arc.

Valet

La Hire.

Valet

Lionel,
enlevant l'épée de Jeanne d'Arc.

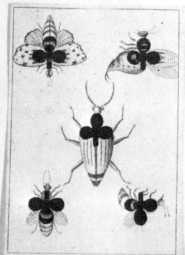

À Tubinge
chez J. G. Cotta, Libraire.

1649 by a family which came from Italy about the beginning of the fifteenth century, issued the first of the transformation, or harlequin cards, as they became known in America. These are cards which have in fact been 'transformed' by so adding to the suit signs, or by drawing the suit signs sideways or even upside down that they form an integral part of a miniature, more often amusing than not. Thus an excellent face can be obtained by adding eyes, a nose and a mouth to a heart. Hearts reversed make fine head-gear. Diamonds can be used for windows, as can spades, or for the wings of fairies. The possible number of transformations is infinite. The results are generally charming, frequently amusing and occasionally dull. These cards are said to have been inspired by the small, leather-bound almanacks which it was the German custom to give away at the New Year, and which had a few engravings into which the suit signs had been ingeniously worked. That the packs were known as *Karten Almanach* supports this theory.

Transformation cards.
Bowes Museum, Durham

In the Cotta series the pip cards only were transformed, the designs, which covered a wide diversity of subjects, being not only independent of one another but also of the value of the cards and of the courts. The untransformed, full-length figures of the latter were designed according to a special theme, a new theme being chosen each year. These packs were issued for the years 1805 to 1808 inclusive and again for the years 1810 and 1811. Why the year 1809 was left out is not known; but the most reasonable supposition is that the management was busy with preparations for the removal of the business to Stuttgart in the following year. In 1805 the courts, designed by Countess Jennison Vallvert, depicted characters from Schiller's play *Die Jungfrau von Orleans*, first performed in 1802 and dealing with Joan of Arc, who is shown on the queen of spades; in 1806 the courts are Ulysses and other figures from classical mythology; in 1807 the designer again turned to Schiller, the theme being taken from the great trilogy *Wallenstein*; in 1808 the subject matter was Arabian costumes; in 1810 mythological figures and caricatures, said to be the work of the Viennese artist C. F. Osiander, who later issued a pack under his own imprint; and in 1811 pictures from the orders of chivalry in which the little known order of Amarantha, instituted by the Queen of Sweden, in the mid-seventeenth century, plays a surprisingly prominent part.

Before the Cotta series came to an end the idea was taken up in England, Austria and France, though not, in the first place, very enthusiastically. In England S. W. Fores, of 50 Piccadilly, London, published, in 1808, a pack with burlesque designs and not very funny captions. The two of spades, for instance, shows a young woman sitting on one side of a small, occasional table, on which lies an empty spectacle case. A cat glares at its mistress with every sign of violent disapproval, and on the other side of the table, not very comfortably seated, is a large person in a dress with short sleeves, a book in hand and spectacles on nose. There are two lines of conversation below, one of which reads 'Now Miss Harriet I'll read you a lesson on Patience'

146

and the other 'Lord, Clunt, you are so tedious'. It is hard to believe
that this caused more than a handful of people to split their sides with
laughter. In 1811 S. & T. Fuller of the Temple of Fancy, Rathbone
Place, London, produced a pack etched and coloured by hand, which
was more amusing than its Piccadilly predecessor; at much the same
time I. L. Cowell designed a pack in which the court cards, some with
animal faces, had a surrounding border of miniature playing cards.
In 1828 E. Olivatte published a pack which was more or less a plagiar-
ism of the Cotta pack of 1806 with the theme of Ulysses; after which
there was a pause, lasting for about twenty years, in the production of
this type of pack by English card masters.

Perhaps the interruption was due to the serious side of card playing,
gambling being heavily underlined at this time and for much the
same period. In 1827 William Crockford, the son of a poor fishmonger,
opened Crockford's Club in King Street, St James's, London. Although
lacking in any sort of physical grace, or any education, Crockford was
able to establish himself in a unique position. When the club was
about to be opened he received 60,000 applications for membership
despite the requirement of an annual subscription of £25. Today that
amount would have the purchasing power of over £200. Only 1200 of
the applicants were selected for membership. The club had the largest
gambling room in the world where enormous sums were lost by high-
born gentlemen and a fortune of £52,000,000 won by the low-born
Crockford. He died in 1844. The original site of Crockford is now
occupied by the Devonshire Club with an annual subscription of £30.

To return to transformation cards, H. F. Müller of Vienna issued

147

three packs, one in 1809, one in 1814 and a third in, probably 1817.
Of these we know the designer of the second pack only, his name,
Johann Neidl, appearing on the ace of hearts. His cards show that he
was a craftsman of ability. Osiander's pack, which reached a high
standard, was published in 1815. His subjects were diverse, the four
kings being the commanders-in-chief of the allied armies in the war
against France—Wellington, Blücher, Kutusoff and Schwartzenburg
—the rest including soldiers fighting, sounding the charge, drinking
and playing cards, duels, mythological events, ladies playing musical
instruments and much else. A couple of packs, at times vulgar and not
very amusing, appeared in Paris in 1819; and the only other transformation pack of this period was that drawn by Count D'Orsay for
Lady Blessington. In the nature of things the last are necessarily pen
and ink sketches drawn round the suit marks of an existing pack.
Forty-nine of the cards have survived and are now in the collection of
the United States Playing Card Company of Cincinnati.

If transformation cards behaved like an herbaceous plant, springing
up, flowering freely and then dying away to bloom again another year,
educational cards conducted themselves like an ancient, ornamental
shrub worn out by a long series of annual flowering. That, indeed, was
exactly the case, and after blossoming again and again during its three
centuries of life the plant weakened and its display became progressively
restricted. A few packs were produced in the first quarter of the
nineteenth century, fewer still in the second quarter, after which they
failed to appear at all. Eventually, after long years of lying fallow, the
shrub again blossomed though in a far less showy form.

148

As a result of his books, such as *Wie Gertrud ihre Kinder Lehrt* (1801), and his twenty-year superintendence of the institute he founded at Yverdon on Lake Neuchâtel, from 1805 to 1825, the great Swiss reformer Johann Heinrich Pestalozzi was the leading educationalist in Europe from the beginning of the century until his death in 1827. In Pestalozzi's view the fundamental fact in the art of education was what he called *Anschauung*, or sense impressions, on which are based all educational requirements. Objects in his hands became the subject of lessons. His pupils were not subjected to lessons about unseen objects. The seeing, handling and reasoning about an object was an *Anschauung*. Playing cards did not meet Pestalozzi's requirements for making direct acquaintance with objects, with the result that as his ideas made headway playing cards as visual aids to teaching fell into disuse. Pestalozzi's ideas were carried on by the German philosopher Herbart, who was in the habit of visiting Pestalozzi while himself a private tutor in Switzerland, and by Froebel, also German, who for two years worked under Pestalozzi at Yverdon.

In this field, and in this century, France was the first country to issue a musical pack and a natural history pack, both published in 1808. Then

Musical cards from an early nineteenth-century German pack.
Bodleian Library, Oxford

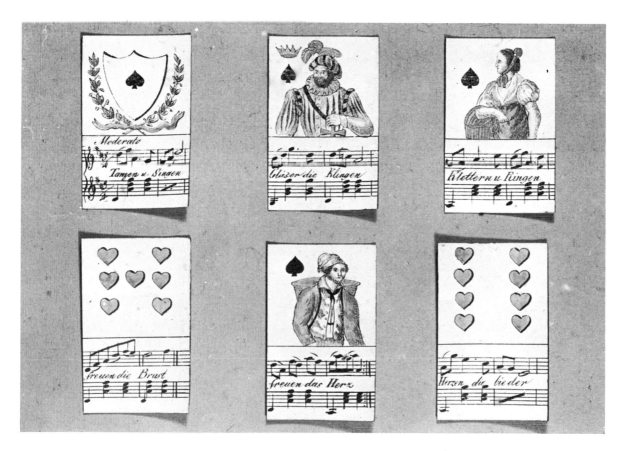

came the United States of America, where two packs of this type, one
geographical and one alphabetical, appeared in 1810. After that Milan
turned out two New Testament packs, one published by P. & G.
Vallardi and one by G. Pirotta, in 1815, following up with a quartet
teaching Grecian history, Roman history, ancient history and geography. The last of these appeared in 1826 and all four were copies of
earlier French packs. In 1820, France published another charming
botany pack which had small coloured drawings of flowers and
vegetables and miniature cards to show the values of the pip cards, an
astronomical pack and, about 1830, an alphabetical pack. The last
shows the letters of the alphabet in large and small type accompanied
by pictures of objects the word for which begins with those letters. At
about this time a well engraved pack with coloured miniature cards in
one corner was offered for sale by a toy shop in Bond Street. Nearly all
the cards give particulars of English kings, queens and dukes, but the
2 to 5 of hearts have engravings of a British Warrior, a Pict, an ancient
Briton and a Druid, and the 2 to 10 of Spades arithmetical tables,
apothecaries, weights and other information. In 1830 Berman of
Vienna printed *Les Cartes Musiciennes* with thirty-two cards each with
music on the bottom half and so arranged that if any eight are laid out
in the order king to 7 a complete waltz results. In 1830 Russia made
her first significant contribution to the playing card scene with a
splendid geographical pack, the charm of which can be gauged from
the fact that Catherine Perry Hargrave devotes two pages of her book
to its description and three pages of illustration. One cannot improve
on her first three paragraphs:

150

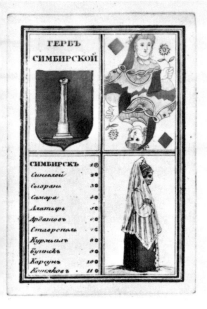

They are beautifully engraved and coloured by hand. Besides the usual fifty-two cards, there are eight extra ones, each showing a map of a part of Russia. On each of the fifty-two cards is the usual suit sign, a small playing card, occupying the upper right-hand corner. The upper left-hand quarter of the card bears the coat of arms of a Russian province; in the quarter below is a list of the principal towns, and in the lower right-hand corner is a figure in the native costume of the province.

They are rich and lovely, these rare little reminders of old imperial Russia. On the excellent little maps, which are faintly tinted in water-colour, the distances between the great cities are

Russian geographical pack depicting two provinces and six towns with arms of the city, 1830.
British Museum

given in versts, St Petersburg and Omsk and Moscow, and many
others.

So much that is lost and gone is recorded on each little card with
its strange Russian words, the vivid symbolism of its gay coat of
arms, and its quaint little figure stepping out of a far land and
time, that they take on almost the importance of archives.

Turning to England, Baker's Eclectic cards for England, Ireland,
Scotland and Wales appeared in 1813. They were 'sold Wholesale and
Retail from the Manufactory at No 2 King Arthur or New Card Court,
York Street, Blackfriars Road', and were also 'to be had from all
respectable Stationers'. They were 'a selection or Eclectic Company of
the Twelve most eminent personages that ever distinguished themselves in their respective countries for their Heroic Deeds and Wisdom'.
In this pack, acorns and swords (double-edged broad swords) replace
spades and clubs, acorns representing England, swords Wales, diamonds Scotland and hearts Ireland. The forty pip cards have ornamented margins, the right hand ones displaying the national emblem,
the left hand one showing in each case a tendril of leaves, and the base
additional plants of the four nations. Thus acorns have oak leaves at the
side with roses at the base, swords have leeks and mistletoe, diamonds
thistles and hearts shamrocks. Larger than usual, they are $4\frac{1}{2} \times 2\frac{3}{4}$
inches, the cards are boldly drawn and beautifully coloured.

In 1820 three educational packs were put on the market; one a
geographical pack; another, *Magna Charta or Knight Errantry*, with which
was supplied 'a synopsis of Chivalry by a Lady'; and the *Kings of
England* in which the cards have in the top left-hand corner the king's
name, in the centre a full length portrait of the king, and at the foot the
dates of the beginning and end of the reign. In 1818 William Darton of
Holborn Hill, London, published *Famous Personages* with the head and
shoulders of the subject of the card occupying most of the space and the
rest given over to textual instruction. There are no suit signs. The
demand for the pack was such that it was re-issued in 1822, 1823, 1824
and 1825, and one cannot help wondering if part of the demand was
created by schoolmasters ordering sufficient packs to supply all their
scholars, or, perhaps, a particular class or classes. Certainly, about this
time two sets of cards were printed 'for the use of Miss Bradley's School,
Priory, Lincoln', one supplying 'an epitome of the history of England'
and one dealing similarly with France. But the cards were in no sense
packs, being simply rectangular pieces of pasteboard with printed
information. England required fifteen cards, France fourteen. There
were no suit signs at all. Nevertheless, it seems probable that Miss
Bradley based her idea on real cards seen in some other school.

In 1828 C. Hodges of 27 Portman Square, London, offered the public
a pack of astronomical playing cards in which the signs of the zodiac
are beautifully represented in charming colours, but which has no

See colour illustration page 113

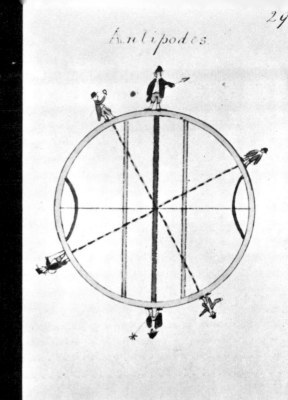

Antipodes.

Heteroscii.

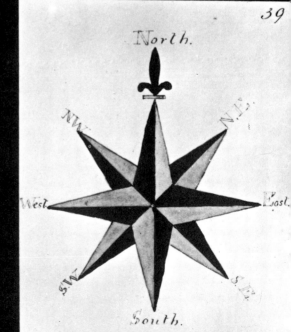

North.

NW. N.E.

West. East.

S.W. S.E.

South.

ANGLETERRE.   FRANCE.   AUTRICHE   RUSSIE.

suit signs. A second edition with suit signs was later sold by Spofforth & Sons of London. In 1836, or thereabouts, *The Royal Historical Game of Cards*, invented by Miss Jane Roberts, was to be seen in the shops. This is a series of forty-five cards with full length portraits of English monarchs from William I to Queen Victoria. Each king and queen, in state robes, stands upon a low pedestal, on the front panel of which is printed his or her name and number, such as Henry VIII and the year, within the century, the reign began—in Henry's case 9. Separate cards list the full accessional details of all the monarchs, century by century. For example, the card for the seventeenth century reads 'James 1st 1603, Charles 1st 1625, Commonwealth 1649, Charles 2nd 1660, James 2nd 1685, William and Mary 1689'. The cards are elegantly printed in bronze powder, and where it applies the king's surname is given. Thus we see William I surnamed the Conqueror; Henry II Curtmantle and Fitzempress; John, Sans Terre, or Lackland; and Edward I, Longshanks.

Up till now the cardboard couples had proved surprisingly fruitful. Their descendents were not only numerous but exceedingly various, some hideous some beautiful, some gay some sober, some rich some poor, some serious some comic. Now the kings and queens were faced with the possibility of even greater fecundity, only to be achieved, alas, at the expense of variety: for 1832 saw the invention of colour printing. However useful and desirable for mankind at large, the new process brought to the royal eyes an outlook as dreary as the prospect of an approaching funeral, since it meant that more and more cards would be churned out mechanically. Though a technical advance it was an artistic retreat. Whatever the admirers of this small branch of the graphic arts may think, the exact similarity of printed packs was enthusiastically received by the gamblers. They had no wish to have their thoughts distracted by admiration of the design. To them the closest attention to cards and players was of vast importance. Inattention might well mean loss.

The inventor of this process with two diametrically opposed values was a maker of straw hats. Certainly he began life as a printer, from which he graduated to newspaper proprietorship. Newspapers failed him: straw hats brought him a modest but precarious living: colour printing was to bring him a fortune. This man of ingenuity was Thomas de la Rue, who in 1832 was granted Royal Letters Patent for 'improvements in making and ornamenting playing cards', the main feature of which lay in the method of registration. By registration is meant the positioning of different colours, the printing of blues and reds and golds in exactly the right place and not even fractionally out of alignment. De la Rue won this race by no more than a short head: for in 1835 an American, who had worked in London for about five years, registered a similar invention: while in 1836 George Baxter, famous for his prints, registered yet a third invention, which was not much different from the other two.

Jeu Impérial c. 1855. French pack of the four empires: England, France, Austria and Russia. By Grimaud. Collection Evelyn Goshawk; photo Peter Kibbles

If the De la Rue invention was bad for the face of the card it was good for the back. Although the backs sometimes carried a simple design, by and large they were plain, mostly white. Applying his system of colour printing to the backs as well as the faces De la Rue achieved several satisfactory results. For one thing the design masked any flaws in the paper, thereby preventing a player from recognizing a card in his opponent's hand: for another, it enabled De la Rue to use cheaper paper. The development, therefore, was good for the pocket of both gamblers and printer. De la Rue was at pains to obtain the finest designs for the backs of his cards, and whereas 'a dissipated man of genius', according to *Chamber's Journal*, 'who, when he could be laid hold of when quite sober, would, for a guinea or so, furnish a design, such as it was. . . .', Thomas de la Rue was quite prepared to pay up to £30 for a single drawing. It was during his search for first class artists who would undertake this work that he became acqainted with Owen Jones, the eminent architect and interior designer, who, over the years, was to create many card-back designs in the intervals of designing and supervising the decorations of the Great Exhibition and other work. De la Rue also introduced improved methods of glazing as well as the use of enamelled paper.

It is interesting that this comparative newcomer to the trade very nearly came to grief with one of his earliest packs. He had the temerity to give his kings and queens and knaves a life-like look, at the same time making their clothes perfectly practical and such as might be worn in actual life. As a more experienced operator would have anticipated, the changes proved unacceptable to the public, and the design had to be withdrawn. Thomas de la Rue is said to have lost heavily on the pack, and those losses were, no doubt, a significant contribution to his near-bankruptcy in 1837. On May 27th of that year he was arrested and locked in a sponging-house, a temporary lodging for an arrested debtor who, it was hoped, would thereby be spurred into settling his affairs and avoiding a prison sentence. Luckily for De la Rue his lawyer obtained his release in a few hours, and such was the resilience of this able man that he went on to discharge his debts and acquire a small fortune. Here we may conveniently mention, though a trifle out of chronological order, three packs which Thomas de la Rue made at the time of the Great Exhibition, in the organizing of which the De la Rues had a big part. Since these cards attracted the attention of none other than the great Charles Dickens himself the description may be left to him.

The blue-bell, the forget-me-not, the daisy, the carnation, the ear of wheat or of barley, all form pretty devices for the backs of cards, as the manufacturers have amply shown. Unless for the highest class of cards, the whole device is in some one colour; but Messrs De La Rue have lately produced cards in which the device at the back is fully coloured in various tints. One set especially, a right royal set of four packs, tells us how imagery has been brought in aid of playing cards. One of these packs has, on every card, the initials V. R. in fanciful letters in the centre of the back; another has P.A., another P.W., and the fourth has P.R. To whom these initials relate it is not difficult to guess; and the exquisite flowers and leaves which are made to intertwine among and around the letters are intended, by a little of the poetry of card-making, to symbolise qualities in the august personages. The rose and the hawthorn surrounding one monogram; the holly, the ivy, and the oak, surrounding another; the fuschia and the daisy, a third; the primrose, the violet, and the lily, a fourth. We will leave those who are learned in the language of flowers to interpret all these symbols, and to apply them to the proper objects; suffice it here to say that Mr Owen Jones has been employed in the production of these very graceful designs and that each card back forms a dainty little picture, worthy of being regarded as such, irrespective of the main purpose of the card.

Though England, in the person of a maker of straw hats, led the way in colour printing, the United States, in the person of a stationer, was not far behind. Lewis I. Cohen, who was born in Pennsylvania in 1800 (De la Rue was born in Guernsey in 1793), came to London in 1814 and worked for his half-brother Solomon Cohen, a manufacturer of lead pencils, for the better part of five years. He then returned to the States. He published his first pack in 1832, printing an arc of thirteen stars above the eagle, itself above the suit sign, on the ace of spades. Presumably the stars represent the number of states originally in the union; but if that indeed be so it is difficult to understand why Cohen sometimes omitted them altogether and on at least one pack printed a total of fourteen. In 1835 he registered his machine for printing four colours at one time, and it is interesting to note that one of his early packs was printed in gold: for Thomas de la Rue had also used that metal, producing a golden New Testament in 1829, and gilding a single edition of the *Sun* newspaper on 28 June 1838, to mark the coronation of Queen Victoria. As if there were not enough similarities already between the careers of Thomas de la Rue and Lewis Cohen, the latter also used back designs by Owen Jones. In 1854 Cohen retired from business, four years before his English rival, leaving his card manufactory in the hands of his son Solomon L. Cohen and his nephew John M. Lawrence, who formed a partnership trading as Lawrence and Cohen.

In 1871 Lawrence and Cohen took three first cousins into their business, which they then converted into a stock company with the style and title of the New York Consolidated Card Company. Two of the cousins were named Levy. The third was Samuel Hart, who had been in business in Philadelphia as a stationer since 1844 and as a card manufacturer since 1849, and who occupies a considerable position in

United States card history by reason of having scored a string of American 'firsts'—double ends, round corners, satin surfaced cards and, possibly, jokers. He was also a pioneer of 'squeezers', which were cards with miniatures in the corners enabling a player to squeeze his hand into a tight, secretive fan and yet know the value of each card.

While De la Rue and Cohen were forging ahead, one on each side of the Atlantic, France was to some extent lagging behind. Lorna Housemann, in *The House That Thomas Built*, quotes a French authority of the time as writing 'De la Rue, Cartier à Londres, a deposé un brevet pour un proçede permettant de colorier les cartes avec les couleurs a l'huile . . . En France ce precede ne sera couramment employé qu'après 1850 environ. . . .' But even if for a while in a state of technical quiessence, in mid-century French card masters produced a series of splendid costume cards. Of these, three printed in Paris were among the finest, one in 1848 by Pierrat, one in 1878 by O. Gibert, and one in 1856 by the well known firm of B. P. Grimaud et Cie. The House of Grimaud was founded in 1748 and was the first, or, at least the first in France to use three sheets of paper in the manufacture of pasteboard. In the first two of the costume packs the figures are in contemporary costume but in the last the full length figures, which are beautifully drawn and coloured by hand, are in the dress of their own times. In the Gibert pack the suit signs are gilt. The kings of the Grimaud pack are Charles VI (1367–1422), Francis I (1494–1547), Henry IV (1553–1610) and Louis XIV (1638–1715).

If the French card masters were uninfluenced by Thomas de la Rue's invention they must, at least, have been aware of his existence, since he had business premises in Paris; though whether they were simply offices for the import of playing cards from his London factory or whether they included a factory is not known. In the Schreiber collection there is a pack in which the ace of spades has its suit mark within an oval frame bearing the inscription Thomas de la Rue & Co., London and Paris: there is another in the De La Rue collection, now the property of Señor Fournier.

If De La Rue's effect on the French was small his influence on the Russians was large: for towards the end of 1842 he brought off a remarkable feat of obtaining the appointment of Superintendent of the Russian Playing Card Monopoly for his brother Paul. Paul, like Thomas, spent his early career in the millinery trade; nor did he leave until a couple of years before setting out for St Petersburg. Thomas himself admitted that the Tsar treated him handsomely for revealing his secrets, and since the London firm supplied St Petersburg with paper, ink, at least one Roller Press (at a price of £130) and spare parts, Paul's appointment was undoubtedly a fine stroke of business for Thomas de la Rue.

The card history of Russia is obscure though in all probability rooted in that of Germany. Also screened from view is the purse into which

Nineteenth-century Russian pack with German suit signs. British Museum

158

ВЪ ПОЛЬЗУ

ВОСПИТ: ДОМА.

the profits of the Playing Card Monopoly finally disappeared. In theory these profits were used for the support of the Foundling Hospital whose seal, incorporating a pelican in her piety, always appeared on the ace of diamonds underneath the Russian eagle. But known, deep seated corruption coupled with the general notion that few successful enterprises escaped the eye of the Tsar renders it unlikely that the Foundlings enjoyed the full benefits of Paul's energy and expertise. In this case rumour may have been unfair to the Tsar: for the Hospital was founded by Catherine the Great at the express wish of Paul when, as a boy, he fell ill of a fever and when getting better requested his imperial Mother to found a hospital for the poor. 'What a heart of gold', murmered Catherine, who immediately granted the request. The foundations were laid the next year, and at the same time a commemorative medal was struck with the inscription 'Himself cured of illness, he remembered the needs of the ailing poor'. In 1800, Paul, as emperor, was struck by the 'Likely injurious consequences to the national morality' of imported books and music and strictly forbade their entry into the country. Not long afterwards it occurred to the Tsar that there was no real need for books at all, Russian or foreign, and he issued an imperial edict closing all the printing presses in Russia with the exception of those belonging to the Synod and Academy of Sciences.

Clearly the business conditions were highly favourable to Paul de la Rue, and that he took every advantage of them is shown by the fact that the output of the Monopoly increased fourfold in the four years to 1847. Despite the immense flow of cards few packs from the period seem to have survived. Catherine Perry Hargrave lists only nine, the geographical one of 1830 apart, as being in the collection of the United States Playing Card Company; the Schreiber collection has three; and the De La Rue collection but one. Such as they are they are charming; and though the evidence on which to base an opinion is thin, it seems that George Clulow was justified in placing Russian cards second only to American in excellence of production. The source of their attraction is not easy to isolate; but undoubtedly the elongation of the points of the spade and club suit marks, and the faces of the courts and their luxurious clothes are most pleasing to the eye.

While the Russian card industry was emerging from a somewhat stagnant past, the card masters of Europe were developing the production of commemoration packs with some success at the same time giving dwindling attention to the educational market. The Germans, in 1834, printed a pack commemorating, through scenes on the four aces, the Portuguese Insurrection of 1820, when the people rose in protest against the appointment of Marshal Beresford to govern the country while their king, who was also of Brazil, took up permanent residence in Rio de Janeiro. Mid-century saw the issue of a royal personage pack by the Belgian firm of Daveluy in which Godefroid de Bouillon (Godfrey of Boulogne) the Belgian Crusader who became king of Jersualem, took the place of the king of hearts, Baudoin de Constantinople that of the king of spades and Charles Quint, Holy Roman Emperor and King of Spain of the king of diamonds. In 1854 a double ended pack, illustrating the Crimean War, was printed in Frankfort. In that pack the aces carried two battle scenes each, the ace of diamonds, for example, having two naval engagements and the ace of clubs vigorous little pictures of the Battles of Alma and Inkermann. The court cards were royalties and generals, those of hearts being Maréchal Pellisier, Eugenie imperatrice, and Napoleon empereur, the first and the last looking much alike, and the king of clubs being Nicolaus I, Czar of Russia, the only royalty to have his title begin with a capital letter. Another Frankfort pack was *Victories of Napoleon*, also double ended and also with two battle scenes on each ace, hearts, for instance, depicting Jena 1806 and Lutzen 1812, and in 1868, still from Frankfort, there appeared a pack depicting the lives of Wellington, Peter the Great, Frederick the Great and Napoleon.

In mid-century the French, who, clearly, were among the last to adopt the principles of Pestalozzi, were responsible for a small series of history packs. The first was a game called *Jeu de Cartes de l'Histoire de France par un Professeur d'Histoire* which became available about 1840. The pack has twelve cards with full length portraits of famous French men and women, such as Charlemagne, Catherine de Medici, Bayard and Bonaparte, taking the place of the courts. Each of the remaining cards has four head and shoulder portraits, painted against a gilt background, of less well known people. None of the figures is very attractive in appearance, with the possible exception of Joan of Arc who has put aside her armour and looks rather appealing. There is some solid, printed instruction on the back of the cards. 1850 saw the arrival of a pack by Gilbert of Paris dealing with personages who may well be eminent so far as the French are concerned but are not so prominent elsewhere. Bussy d'amboise and the Dame de Monsoreau are the king and queen of hearts, the Comte de Brissac and Diane de Boitiers (Mistress of Henry II) are the monarchs of spades, the Chevalier d'Eon (who spent most of his life dressed as a woman) and the Comtesse de Rochfort of diamonds, and Cinq Mars and Marion Delorme of clubs. The suit signs are in gilt and the backs are a splendid Cambridge blue. This pack was followed by two dealing with British historical characters, one by Gilbert and one by Avril, also of Paris, and both packs alike except that Gilbert kept to gilt suit signs for the pip cards.

Elesewhere in Europe, Austria, in 1838, printed a pack of card-maps, one of which showed the United States with twenty-five states and a population of 11,000,000. This was followed by two packs of the Crimean War, one printed *c.* 1854 by Segeder of Vienna and the other, only a year or two later, a tarot pack with *atouts* devoted to the same subject. About 1872 Fulladosa y Ca of Barcelona published a pack with court cards showing eminent Spaniards from the fourteenth century onwards and is remarkable among Spanish cards for having queens. The English contributed several commemorative packs, one by De La Rue in 1874, the year of the marriage of the Duke of Edinburgh to HRH The Grande Duchess Marie of Russia; one each by De La Rue and Goodall & Sons, to celebrate Queen Victoria's Golden Jubilee in 1887: three, by De La Rue, Goodall & Sons and the Kimberley Press of Birmingham, on the occasion of the Queen's Diamond Jubilee in 1897; and one by Waddington in 1893 to mark the wedding of the future King George V and Queen Mary. The 1874 pack was of more than usual interest. Designed by Reuben Townroe for Felix Summerley's Art Manufacturers and printed by De La Rue, it was planned as an international pack rather than a commemoration of the royal event, and to that end the backs had the English Royal Arms over the double headed eagle of Prussia, both in gold, printed on a blue, alternatively red, background. The aces had the portraits of Queen Victoria Empress of India, the President of the United States of America, the Czar of Russia and the Emperor of Germany. The queens were the Princess of Wales, the Empress of Austria, the Queen of Greece and the Crown Princess of Germany. It was not particularly successful. The pack put out by the Kimberley Press was sold as *Royal National Patriotic Cards*, and seem to have been the only cards produced by that firm. In the year 1886 one of the very few Scottish packs came into the world. This was a photolithographic copy of the old *Rump Parliament* pack, issued in the seventeenth century, and was specially produced for the Aungervyle Society by E. E. Goldsmith of Edinburgh. Finally we must mention a noted German pack which was

See colour illustration page 128

published by Dondorf in the 1890s under the name of *Luxus Spielkarten*, often translated as *The Four Corners of the World Pack*. It has been given the latter title because each of its suits represents a continent, and each of the pip cards has a scene related to the history of its particular continent with a title printed either at the side or the foot. Spades are the suit of Africa, the courts being the Sultan, the Sultana (apparently, but not named) and a Janizary. Hearts stand for Asia and have The Great Mogul, a Hindoo Princess and a Hindoo warrior for court cards. Diamonds are for Europe with the Emperor and Empress as king and queen and a lance bearer as the knave, while clubs stand for America with, curiously enough, Ferdinand and Isabella and a Spanish Ambassador for courts, with pictures of Columbus and his sailors discovering America, preparing defences against the Indians and of the various birds and beasts indigenous to the newly discovered territory. The backs have a design showing a woman with flowing draperies poised on one foot on a globe against Highland scenery of lochs and hills.

The second half of the century saw a revival in the fortunes of transformation packs. Round about 1860 Samuel Hart produced a pack of this kind with designs originally published in England by William Tegg about ten years earlier, and in the intervening decade

copied in Vienna and Munich. His example was followed in 1876 by F. H. Lowerre of New York who published the *Eclipse Comic Playing Cards*, and in 1879 by Tiffany and Company of New York who printed cards to designs by C. E. Carryl and which, in the view of some people, are the best American cards of their kind. In 1895 The United States Playing Card Company marketed the *Hustling Joe* and *Vanity Fair* packs, both well known and successful but not really transformation packs in that the amusing faces of the cards were superimposed upon the suit signs which were left untouched. In the meantime France was responsible for a transformation pack dealing with Jeanne d'Arc which appeared about 1860 and was produced by lithography; while in England a pack designed by Chapman was issued by Reynolds & Sons and another by an unknown artist printed *c.* 1865 by Maclure, Macdonald and Macgregor of Market St, Manchester. The *Orphans of Pimlico* being 'Sketches, Fragments and Drawings' by Thackeray, gathered together and published after his death by his daughter, contained twenty-one transformations drawn by the great author himself.

The same period saw a general burgeoning of playing card production in North America. In the United States at least fifty new firms started in business, five or six appeared in Canada, including the Union Card and Paper Co. of Montreal which printed the first Canadian joker in 1887, and three or four in Mexico. The Americans poured out packs from a score or more states, all but three of which — made up of one in each of the states of Montana, California and Washington—were in the eastern half of the country. It is not possible to mention more than a few of the more interesting cards.

About 1875 Andrew Dougherty, who had begun manufacturing

The Four Continents 1880. Pip cards, each suit representing a continent: hearts Asia, clubs America, diamonds Europe and spades Africa. Collection Evelyn Goshawk; photo Peter Kibbles See also page 128 (colour)

163

You will need help.

164

playing cards in 1842 and who was to become an outstanding figure in the trade, published 'triplicate' cards, that is cards indexed with miniature cards in two opposing corners, in direct competition with squeezers made by Lawrence and Cohen's New York Consolidated Card Company. The two companies came to a sales agreement dividing the States into two parts in the manner of the Pope dividing the New World—the East Indies to Portugal and the West Indies Spain. In 1874 the Globe Company of Boston published the first American pack of round cards, in which the club suit is printed in green, the diamond in yellow and the other two in red. In 1881 Russell, Morgan and Company issued their first cards, Capitol packs, in which the court cards are essentially English in appearance. Ten years later this company changed its name to The United States Printing Company and in 1894 to the United States Playing Card Company which has since achieved a dominating position in the trade. It was this company that adopted the bicycle trademark, so familiar in the States. At about this time The Waterproof Card Company of Boston issued a pack of circular cards, while in 1885 small cards were enclosed in packets of cigarettes, becoming the first advertising playing cards. In 1889 The Kenney Tobacco Company reissued the *Tiffany* pack with Carryl designs in the form of cigarette cards. The World's Columbian Exposition, held in 1893 in Chicago to celebrate the 400th anniversary of the discovery of America by Christopher Columbus, was the raison d'être for two souvenir packs. All the courts of one of of the packs had head and shoulder portraits of Colonel George Davis, Director General of the Fair, Mrs Potter Palmer, wife of a noted store proprietor and realtor, and society leader who had been appointed President of the Board of Lady Managers, and, almost forgotten among such important folk, and suitably humbled as a knave, none other than Christopher Columbus himself. In the other pack two miniature cards at opposite corners indicated the values, and Columbus appeared on an extra card.

But perhaps the most interesting series of this period is that formed by the packs issued during the Civil War. In 1862 The American Card Company of New York put out a *Union* pack in which the suits are stars, flags, shields and eagles, the kings are colonels, the queens the Goddess of Liberty and the knaves majors; the next year M. Nelson of New York published a *Union Generals* pack and in 1865, with fine impartiality, a *Confederate Generals* pack; and in 1865 Andrew Dougherty issued a *Monitor* and *Merrimac* pack, officially called *Army and Navy Cards*, in which the suit signs are zouaves and drummer boys in the red suits and the *Monitor* and *Merrimac* in the blue. The Monitor was a Union battleship which fought the Confederate Merrimac in the drawn Battle of Hampton Roads in 1862. In 1863 Charles Goodall & Sons joined in the game by printing in London, and selling in the States through their New York office, a pack with backs decorated with Confederate flags. The main interest of all these cards lies not so

Card from a fortune telling pack, *c.* 1860. Bowes Museum, Durham, and Collection Peter Gowans

165

4 TU-WHIT TU-WHO

4

WEG DRUMMING.

2 CAW-CAW

HEE-HAW

1

1 Find Peg and Sarah Jane L.C.

THE GOLLIWOGG.

much in the cards themselves as in the fact that they were printed during the course of the war and not as commemorative packs later. This was a practice taken up with vigour during the first and second world wars.

During this rich American harvest, England seems to have been more concerned with the technical problems of production and the procurement of attractive back designs than with the development of the face. Before the first half of the century had passed, De La Rue, thanks to the Founder's invention and the mechanical ability of his elder son, Warren, was in the happy position of selling more than one hundred thousand packs a year—sales on top, of course, of those of their manifold stationery interests. Warren de la Rue was a Fellow of the Royal Society, and at different times was President of the Royal Chemical Society, the Royal Astronomical Society and the London Institution. With their closest rivals, Charles Goodall & Sons, the firm of De La Rue enjoyed about sixty per cent of the English market. But the capacity of their machinery was far from absorbed and they were constantly looking round for new outlets. Railway tickets were among the first of their side lines, and were a splendid outlet since they not only kept the presses working but used up waste from the card department. Visiting-cards were another useful outlet. In 1855 De La Rue were awarded their first postage stamp contract, the forerunner of many. With so many other interests it is not surprising that their production of special packs of playing cards was limited.

The changes in the cards themselves, as opposed to the design of their faces, included the introduction of round corners and indices somewhere about 1870 (De La Rue), pneumatic finish to facilitate dealing and handling generally (invented by Thomas Shaw, a partner in De La Rue), double ended cards as a standard practice (Banckes & Co) and waterproof cards (tried out by Perry & Co). In 1880 James

Children's Games: *Animal Grab* and *Golliwog*, by de la Rue, *c.* 1900
Gunnersbury Park Museum, London

English multiplication table game: *Laugh and Lay Down*, nineteenth century.
British Museum

167

The Queen by Evans and Sons, *c.* 1855. Printed by the Kronheim process, a form of lithography. Suits are crowns, fleurs de lis, mitres and Garter stars.

Bowes Museum, Durham

English & Co. made Anglo-American Squeezers, presumably under licence from the States. But perhaps the main feature of this period in England was the great output of children's games. *Nursery Rhyme*, *Happy Families*, and *Animal Grab* were among those offered by De La Rue; *Game of the Bride*, *Illustrated Proverbs* and *Laughing made Easy* were sold by Jaques & Co., a notable business in the toy and games trade, and a host of others. Another feature of the last quarter of a century was the commencement, in the year 1882, of the series of packs specially printed for the annual inauguration banquet of the New Master and Wardens of the Worshipful Company of Makers of Playing Cards. In these packs a portrait of the Master appears on the ace of spades whilst the backs have a picture of one of the more important events of the year. Normally the arms of the Worshipful Company are superimposed, faintly, upon a corner of the picture. Since 1896 a prize, known as the 'H. D. Phillips Prize', after the Master at the time of the Diamond Jubilee, has been offered for the best design. The close of the century also saw the introduction of cards for the blind, a German development of the 1880s. These are achieved by printing Braille dots beside the indices.

All forms of art, even down to this small branch, have their erotica, and playing cards have not escaped. In the middle of the nineteenth century the French took to printing what are known as translucent or transparent cards. Although they appear to be normal cards when spread out on a table or handled in the usual way, when held up to the light they reveal the sort of picture which in the past was generally associated with the docks at Port Said. In common with most erotica they tend to go underground, and though a good many were printed they are not often seen. Transparent cards which were vulgar, rather than erotic, were made by The Transparent Playing Card Company of New York.

Pack designed by Jean Picart le Doux to celebrate the 125th anniversary of the De La Rue Company, 1957

The twentieth century

18 de JULIO
Por Dios, la Patria y el Rey

Artistic backs.
Collection Evelyn Goshawk;
photo Peter Kibbles

Even before the arrival of the twentieth century, the attitude of card makers to their product had changed. Cards were no longer the fruits of one of the minor arts but the end product of batteries of machines. Output per factor of production, and the volume of sales required to keep the machines and their automatic paper feeders working at full blast, rather than the artistry of craftsmen, were the dominant questions in the minds of Presidents, Vice-Presidents and Managing Directors. With chromolithography, photography and the most modern techniques pressed into service quantity production was easily obtained. Commemoration packs, education packs, war packs, Coronation packs, and just plain packs streamed from the presses: back designs multiplied and increased, birds and beasts, fishes and flowers, pin-up beauties and bathing beauties, steamships and railroads, miniature cards and midget cards, cards advertising all sorts and kinds of goods and services showered down upon the world in much the same way that the pack flew down upon Alice when she cried out 'Who cares about you?' The small card manufactory was pushed out of business. Masters perforce hired themselves out as employees; craftsmen gave way to operatives; individuality was submerged in the mass. The standard designs became unchangeable, partly because the most economic use of the machines required immensely long runs and partly because the faces and poses and costumes of the courts and the arrangement of the suit signs had become internationalized. More players in more countries resented any change. The cardboard kings and queens and knaves were perforce preserved like larks in aspic or peaches in brandy.

The century opened with one war in progress and one a very green memory. In February 1898 the USS Maine was blown up in Havana harbour, loudly proclaiming the beginning of the Spanish American War. The New York Consolidated Card Company manufactured, specially for the troops, cards packed in a 'knapsack', as they termed the carton, which had a roll of dice at the top. It is doubtful if this was a profitable venture since, except for General Shafter's forces which captured Santiago, the war was fought entirely at sea. Two years later, by which time the fighting had ceased, and a peace treaty had been signed, The United States Playing Card Company published an *Army and Navy* pack, with American heroes from the war as courts, as an advertisement for the Anheuser-Busch Brewery. It had a picture of the brewery on all the pip cards. In the meantime the English in South Africa had been attacked by the Boers, the first action of the South

African War being fought on 10 October 1899. The following year, C. L. Wüst of Frankfort, whose sympathies clearly lay with the Boers, published a pack in which Kruger, four times President of the South African Republic, and General Cronje, who defeated the British at the Battle of the Modder River and again at Magersfontein, appeared among the kings. A more interesting pack to come out of this was the one made by H. M. Guest at a time when guerilla warfare had created a shortage of all manner of goods, not least playing cards. Printed on rough paper from blocks carved by Guest (Newspaper proprietor of Klerksdorp, Transvaal, and wartime Reuter's representative) with the help of a friend, the result, while necessarily amateur, is amusing and has a charm acquired from the difficulties attendent upon its birth. The Worshipful Company filled the gap between these two wars and the first world war by commemorating the centenary of the Battle of Trafalgar (1805) with a pack with a picture of Nelson and the Battle on the backs. It was printed by C. Goodall & Sons.

In 1901 Queen Victoria died and was succeeded on the English throne by Edward VII, who was crowned the following year. De La Rue marked the occasion by bringing out a coronation pack, the backs of which had a crown in the centre and emblems of the Commonwealth in the four corners. When King Edward, in his turn, died, both Waddington and Goodall & Sons produced special packs for the coronation of the next monarch, George V, Waddington also printing an additional, quite separate pack for the crowning of Queen Mary, the queen consort.

In the opening years of the new century a trickle of souvenir packs for the tripper and the tourist came from the American presses. In 1900, for instance, The United States Playing Card Company printed souvenir packs of Washington, DC, and the *White Pass and Yukon Route;* in 1901 Hawaiian, Californian and Niagara Falls souvenir packs were published; and so it went on, the trickle becoming, with time, a stream and the stream a mighty river with tributaries from every card producing country in the world. There were Panama, East Coast of Florida, Picturesque Canada, Brighton (England), Wisconsin, Copenhagen, Montreal, Ireland (by the Ormond Printing Company of Dublin), Colorful Colorado, Lille, Beautiful Britain, Isle of Man, Nevada, Bermuda, Joyaux en Belgique, Mexican Monuments, Norwegian, Spanish and New Zealand souvenirs, and that is but scratching the vast field of pasteboard mementos. Nor were the shipping lines, the rail roads, and, later, the airlines which connected all these far scattered places, indifferent to the advantages of this type of advertising, and they, too, were soon printing their own souvenir packs. Mostly these cards are a tribute to the high standards of photography and printing of their times rather than to originality or art.

The great chorus of keepsake cards, of one sort or another, occupying the centre of the stage should not deter the eye from the action in the

English Political Pack of 1886 by Willis & Co. Portraits of Healy, Hartington, Dilke, Parnell, Chamberlain and Churchill, politicians concerned in the struggle for Irish Home Rule.
British Museum

wings. There we may see the great firm of Heraclio Fournier of Vitoria, Spain, making its entry, in the year 1900, with a superb costume pack. Printing and playing cards must have long been among the family interests, since in the mid-eighteenth century P. S. Fournier le Jeune was corresponding at length with J. G. I. Breitkopf, author of one of the earliest books on playing cards, on the subject of 'the new manner of printing music'. Was Braucio Fournier of Burgos who printed a pack with 'Carol. III D. G. Hispa. Ind R 1805' on all coins a member of the family? Again in 1901, The Aluminium Manufacturing Company of Wisconsin experimented with a pack of aluminium cards, the lithographed fronts and backs being pasted on to thin sheets of that metal. The weight of the pack was five ounces, far different from an iron pack attempted in the middle of the previous century by Johann Najedly of Vienna, which has been estimated to have weighed one pound two ounces. In the other wing two packs have good entertainment value. One, produced in the first decade of the century as an advertising pack, had the Presidents of the United States as kings and jokers and their First Ladies as queens. It is known as *The President Suspender Deck* since each and every one of the figures wears 'suspenders'. The other pack is *The Women are Trumps Deck*, invented by Mrs John King Van Renselaer who wtote, in the 1890s, two books about playing cards. The suits in this pack are crowns, bells, serpents and Maltese crosses, and each card has a black and white figure of a distinguished woman over a short biographical note. In the crown suit the women are chosen from royalty, in the bell suit from prominent ladies of the United States, in serpents from well known ladies of other

A French nineteenth-century game portraying the idiosyncrasies of English, French, German and American national characters. Collection Evelyn Goshawk; photo Peter Kibbles

GRETCHEN MICHEL

Madame MICHEL

HARRY JOHN BULL

JOHN BULL

Monsieur JOSEPH PRUDHOMME

Madame PRUDHOMME

JONATHAN

Mistress JONATHAN

BARRERA

GITANILLO

R. TORRES

JUAN DÍAZ DE SOLÍS
Descubre el Río de la Plata, 1516

GIL GONZÁLEZ DÁVILA
Descubre Costa Rica, Nicaragua y Honduras, 1523

HERNÁN CORTÉS
Conquistador de México, 1519

countries, and in Maltese crosses from the world's oppressed. This unusual pack was published in 1914 by The Bailey, Banks, Middle Company of Philadelphia.

The first world war offered a considerable opportunity to the card makers of the world. Mostly they seized it. In general, whether from Triple Alliance or Allied countries, the packs had pictures of heads of State and outstanding generals on the courts and action scenes on the other cards. German packs, as was only to be expected, displayed the Kaiser and Hindenberg and Tirpitz. Piatnik u. Söhne of Vienna, founded in the middle of the nineteenth century and today one of the leading European firms, brought out a complete tarot pack with the trumps given up to war pictures. The Montreal Lithograph Co. disdaining any narrow, national view, produced a pack which showed kings and generals and private soldiers of the Allied Forces and had no less than six national flags on the backs. De La Rue and Goodall & Sons took much the same line in England, the latter including in its three packs, to De La Rue's two, *Fragments* by Bruce Bairnsfather, which was an effort to get away from the common run. Because of the law of their land, which required adherence to the standard design, France took no part in these activities, though she printed patriotic children's games which were not legally controlled in the same way. In 1915, 1917 and 1918 the United States produced war packs which were fervently democratic and shouted 'down' with kings and 'up' with democracy, while the United States Playing Card Company put out in the last year of the war a French educational game with French and English phrases on each card, together with instructions on pronun-

The White Pass and Yukon Route, Souvenir pack 1900. Collection Evelyn Goshawk; photo Peter Kibbles

ciation, for the benefit of troops stationed in Europe. Just after the war Belgium printed a double, victory pack, yet again with pictures of heads of State, generals and battle scenes.

In the second world war the pattern of the first was to all intents and purposes repeated. In 1943 Biermans of Turnhour, Belgium, issues a *Jeep* pack in anticipation of liberation. It has jeeps on the back, and on the aces heads of Stalin, Montgomery, Eisenhower and de Gaulle. The Universal Playing Card Co, previously known as Alf Cooke & Co. published a *Victory* pack in 1944, which had portraits of Allied leaders, including Roosevelt and Stalin, on the backs over the motto 'United We Stand'; and in the very same year Belgium issued a pack with the motto 'Union Fait La Force' and pictures of the Allied leaders. Churchill was drawn as the king of spades, Roosevelt as the king of diamonds, Stalin as the king of hearts, and de Gaulle as king of clubs. Hitler takes the part of a joker and is shown with a bomb dropping on his head. In 1941 The E. E. Fairchild Corporation, of Rochester, New York, printed a *Bundles for Britain* pack, with a golden lion and shield on the back below which appeared the initials B.W.R.S. The United States Playing Card Company issued a *Relief for Yugoslavia* pack with the Yugoslav crest in gold on the back, and an American *Friends of Norway* pack, also with the national crest in gold on the back. Waddingtons of Leeds issued a special pack to commemorate the gallant landing by the First Allied Airborne Division at Arnhem in September 1944. The United States Playing Card Company issued a *Spotter* pack designed to teach aircraft recognition, spades and hearts showing United States and English planes respectively, and diamonds and clubs German and Japanese planes respectively. The Arrco Playing

Card Company of Chicago produced a *Victory* pack with Uncle Sam, Miss Liberty and soldiers and sailors for courts, and in 1943 Burton Crane issued a *French Lingo* pack, to help American servicemen to learn French, which had 108 cards with five phrases on each card. In 1941 Germany made fun of her enemies with a pack showing the leaders of the Allies in undignified positions and in 1940 Japan put out a sixty-card military pack with pictures of officers, men, and battleships and aeroplanes.

War apart, the accent in the last five decades seems to be on a search for novelty rather than any attempt at development. John Waddington of Leeds tried circular cards in the 1920s, barrel shaped cards in the 1950s and Zulu shield shaped cards in 1959. Grandmother Stover's Inc, of Columbus, Ohio, published cards $\frac{5}{16} \times \frac{3}{4}$ inches, and the United States Playing Card Company a jumbo pack with cards $7 \times 4\frac{1}{2}$ inches. In the 1920s the Arpak Playing Card Co. of Liverpool printed a pack with black faces on which were yellow spades, green clubs, red hearts and white diamonds, a combination which they thought would prevent confusion, whilst The Avoid Playing Card Company of Virginia tried a pack with spades printed in black, hearts in red, clubs in purple and diamonds in orange, which, they claimed, would enable players to 'avoid errors, reneges, misplays and eye strain'. De La Rue in 1935, and The United States Playing Card Company in 1938, both tried five suited bridge, and The Double Action Playing Card Company of New York printed cards divided diagonally, half being white and half blue, with a different card on each half. After its Declaration of Independence in 1961, the Republic of South Africa adopted suits of cart wheels, tent pegs, shoes and powder horns with court cards consisting of boer, vrou and kommandant and president replacing the ace.

Finland and Iceland, Latvia and Bulgaria, Greece and Turkey, Mexico and Uruguay, Cuba and Egypt, Japan and Hong Kong, Brazil and The Argentine, Australia and New Zealand all now print playing cards, and, indeed, there are very few countries that do not. Israel prints Bible cards with David as the king of diamonds, Mexico prints cards with vivid pictures of bull fights, and Russia cards for anti-religious propaganda. Elizabeth II's coronation, Olympic Games, a Playing Card Exhibition in Belgium, and deaf mutes have all been remembered, as have 'The Amalgamated Meat Cutters and Butcher Workmen of North America, A.F. of L.' whose commemorative pack has a picture of Samuel Gompers on the ace of hearts, one of Heywood Brown on the jack of hearts and one of the headquarters building in glorious technicolour on the backs. Back designs have flourished and multiplied and, indeed, little else could be expected when tens of millions of packs are sold annually in the United States alone.

Though packs, back designs, and profits may swell the card masters decrease. According to the *Sunday Times* of 24 February 1969, there were at that date but five card manufacturers in the States out of more

than 200 founded in the previous century. Those five are The United States Playing Card Company of Cincinnati, the Arrco Playing Card Company of Chicago, Stancraft of St Paul, Minnesota, Whitman of Racine, Wisconsin and Kem of Poughkeepsie, New York State. Of these the greatest is The United States Playing Card Company, with more than half the home market, now taken over by The Diamond International Corporation of New York. In Europe, *The Times* of London for 12 May 1963 reported an amalgamation of the playing card manufacturing activities of John Waddington of Leeds, Thomas De La Rue & Co. of London and B. P. Grimaud et Cie of Paris, with M. Jean-Marie Simon of the last company joining Mr Victor Watson of Waddingtons and Mr Peter Orchard of De La Rue on the board of a new Company called The Amalgamated Playing Card Company. The De La Rue playing card collection, together with a unique group of original drawings for back designs, many by well known artists, was sold at auction in November 1970. The catalogue was sadly marred by mis-spellings.

But fewer card masters does not mean that the end of playing cards is in sight or even over the horizon. So long as a Chinaman wishes to play poker with an American, or a Russian piquet with an Egyptian, or Englishmen bridge with Uruguayans or any other combination of people engage in any other game the output of cards must be maintained, if not increased, even if the cards must be made to a standard, international design. With the exception of special packs made in small quantities, it would appear that there is now little chance of the faces of the cards changing, let alone developing. The kings and queens and knaves seem to have reached the final stage in their evolution and presumably will now remain preserved in clothes and attitudes of the past like the Beefeaters at the Tower of London or the Swiss Guards at the Vatican. Over the centuries they have patiently comforted man when bored, entertained him when sociable, afforded excitement when in the gambling mood, instructed him when he needed to learn, and provided space for propaganda when he wanted to state a case. For such immense services over so long a period, and which bid fair to be rendered for further centuries, we cannot withold our profound thanks.

Portuguese playing cards and their journeys

Appendix 1 by Sylvia Mann

Although playing cards of many nations have spread beyond the bounds of their original homeland for a variety of reasons, those of Portugal had, perhaps, the most remarkable history of all. It is understandable how, in this age of rapid communication, the Anglo-American type of card came to be used in most parts of the world, principally for Poker and Bridge, but it must be remembered that the spread of Portuguese cards took place strictly in the age of sail and horse.

The fifteenth- and sixteenth-century voyages of exploration undertaken by the Portuguese coincided with the rapid spread of popularity of cards in Europe, and it is hardly surprising that sailors on long and (however uncertain) tedious journeys took with them the most portable and versatile form of entertainment yet devised. Many of the voyages were concerned principally with trading and resulted in friendly intercourse and exchange of customs with the nations visited: some remarkable evidence of these exchanges have survived in the form of playing cards.

Originally Portuguese packs had forty-eight cards with their own version of the Italian suitmarks of cups, swords, money (or gold) and batons. In addition they had several distinctive features, the two most important being as follows: the court comprised a king, cavalier and female jack called a *sota*, and a dragon or serpent (supporter of the royal Portuguese coat of arms) was depicted on each of the aces. With one exception (and this applies to the *sota* feature only) these characteristics were present on Portuguese-derived cards throughout the world, however much their appearance differed in other respects.

The design of the first cards to travel from Portugal probably closely resembled those illustrated on page 182, because cards made in Japan at the end of the sixteenth century are known which have almost identical designs except that the faces of the court figures have oriental features. Probably in the same century the cards also became established and copied in Brazil, India, Java and Celebes. So far the search has been in vain for evidence of the cards being used in East Africa, Malacca and Macao: there are possible reasons for this such as the Africans not being notable card players, Malacca being so strongly Muslim that card-playing was forbidden and Macao being so close to China, a country notorious for not copying anybody else's customs. However, the possibility must exist that the cards may have been used in these places also.

In Brazil, where the Portuguese remained in control for centuries,

Ace of swords from a Portuguese pack, *c.* 1650. Collection Sylvia Mann

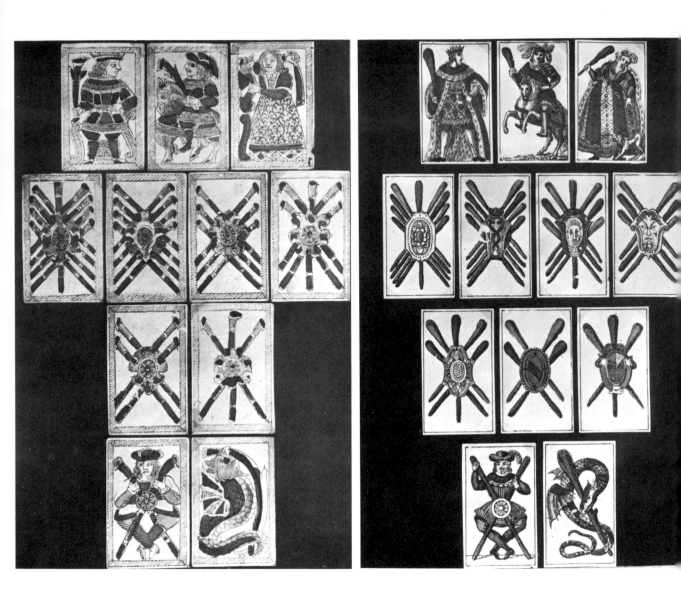

the design of the pack developed alongside that used in the mother country and finally became the rather debased version exemplified above right. This was the style employed at the time of the last known examples of the cards to have been used in Portugal itself, made by the Royal Printing Manufactory in Lisbon in the early nineteenth century. Production continued elsewhere, in Brazil itself, and various exporting centres in Europe such as Nuremberg and Turnhout, probably until the end of the century. Nowadays the cards seem entirely forgotten in Portugal and the female figure once designated the lowly, *sota*, has had her title promoted to that of queen in French-suited packs.

In the East, however, the history of Portuguese-derived cards took quite a different course, one much more exotic and of wider interest. At the beginning of the seventeenth century the Dutch replaced the Portuguese as dominant traders and colonists in many areas, but although the Portuguese themselves departed, many of their customs including playing cards and games remained. These became so absorbed into local culture and tradition that modifications of design resulting from regional art styles can everywhere be observed.

Some examples of native artistic traditions incorporated in local versions of the cards are extremely interesting, whether they are used to decorate beautiful hand-painted packs or result in quickly-produced cards bearing the minimum of line required for easy identification, necessarily crude in appearance. Both Japan and Java have provided examples of these categories.

In the particular area under consideration, the Portuguese came first to India which has bequeathed to posterity fewer examples of Portuguese-derived cards than anywhere else. The earliest known pack, probably of the seventeenth century or possibly earlier, is one which was discovered by the late Dr Martin von Hase. It would, if complete, comprise forty cards which normally one associates with the size of pack used for playing the ancient game of *Ombre*. (A Portuguese adventurer captured by the Chinese in 1533 wished he had the opportunity to play at *Ombre*.) However, this pack is rather different in that it must have been used for some other kind of game (such as baccarat) for the four series of ten cards usually made in separate suits are here four identical series made up of a king, cavalier, *sota*, 7 of batons, 6 of money, 5 of cups, 4 of batons, 3 of swords, 2 of money and an ace of swords bearing the customary dragon. An interesting feature is the replacement of the usual club or baton by an Indian club with a rounded end: this feature is incorporated in all surviving Indian packs, but it is not known elsewhere.

Dr von Hase's cards were crudely made and in European style, apart from the local costume worn by the *sota* figure, but later Indian packs were all made by processes customary to the country: they were hand-painted or lacquered on various substances, including ivory, and all figures wore Indian costume: unlike the early cards, they had four separate suits. In common with a majority of national Indian cards, a female figure does not appear in these packs so that the lowest court card in Indian Portuguese-derived packs is shown as a male.

Java might be said to be next on the Portuguese route to the Far East, so far as cards are concerned. It would appear that *Ombre* became the most popular game and survived there until this century, the Javanese packs all comprising forty cards. Local art traditions make great use of natural history subjects, and in a most beautifully executed pack of *c.* 1700 (now belonging to the Deutsches Spielkarten Museum in Bielefeld), animals, birds and flowers abound intertwined with the suitmarks on the numeral cards. A nineteenth-century pack in the British Museum, with delightful contemporary European figures on

Brazilian cards of the baton suit of *c.* 1840, made by Luis Schlicting of Rio de Janeiro. These are similar to contemporary Portuguese cards and many features are descended from those found on the older cards.
Collection Sylvia Mann

Ace of swords from a mid-nineteenth century pack made by Luis Schlicting of Rio de Janeiro.
Collection Sylvia Mann

The cups suit of a nineteenth-century pack from Celebes, crudely produced in the manner of Toradja art. In common with Japanese cards, the suit sign for cups has been inverted, the form clearly meaning nothing to those who copied the originals.
Collection Sylvia Mann

The court cards from the enlarged form of Portuguese-derived pack invented in Japan and known as *Unsun karuta*. These were hand-painted on a gold background and were made in *c.* 1765. The cards are the *Rohai* (dragon) and *Sōta* (female jack) of the cup suit.
Collection Sylvia Mann

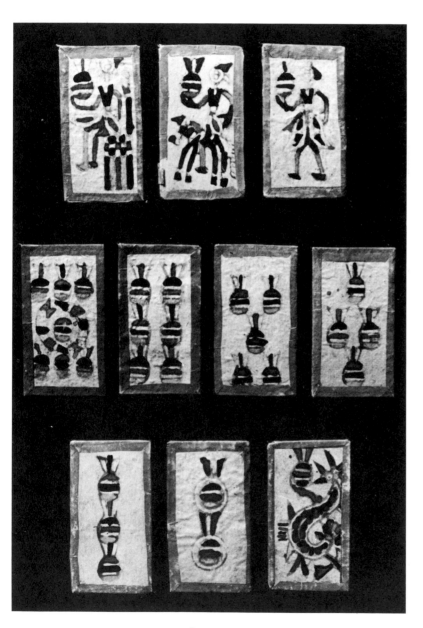

the court cards, has similar features but a vastly inferior artist.

A more usual type of pack, however, would be a cheaply produced model of such crudity that one can more easily wonder at it than admire. In neighbouring Celebes, the Toradja tribes of the interior, whose artistic tradition is simplicity itself, also produced the cards in a style reflected on page 184. The court figures, although hardly recognizable, are distinctively different from each other, and in a way one is reminded of the outlines of the Wayang puppets from neighbouring Java. Needless to say, some sort of dragon decorated all the aces.

A point of interest to note is that whereas Chinese money-cards became the most often used cards in Indonesia, the word for cards is *kertu*, presumably derived from the Portuguese or Dutch words. The Chinese cards are called *kertu china* or *kertu chilik* (little cards) and European derived ones are known as *kertu gedé* or big cards. The local word for a pack of cards is *setel*, equally obviously taken from the Dutch *stel*. It seems curious that with their ancient tradition of card-playing and trading with the Indies that the Chinese did not introduce cards before the Europeans.

It has already been mentioned that the cards with dragons on their aces are no longer used in their homeland or Brazil: there is, however, one country where they are still made and used in upward of a dozen regional styles, and that is Japan. After nearly four hundred years of development, suppression, re-appearance and modification it is not surprising that those who are not initiates into the games played with them may find some of the cards difficult to associate with their European prototypes: but the fact remains that they are still there, and that the history leading up to their survival, although necessarily conjectural from time to time, is an extraordinary one.

When the Portuguese came to Japan in the mid-sixteenth century they were known as the *Nambanjin* or Southern Barbarians. The Japanese were fascinated by the strangers and adopted many *Namban* customs and designs, as well as incorporating many *Namban* words in their vocabulary. Art, food, medicine, dress and social customs (including playing at cards) became part of high fashion, and in 1582 the Japanese even sent a party of envoys to Europe to find out more concerning the background of their visitors. It was probably at about this time in fact, that cards became accepted in fashionable Japan, because the earliest known Portuguese-derived cards were called *Tenshŏ-karuta*, that is cards of the Tenshŏ period which lasted from 1573 to 1592.

These *Tenshŏ-karuta* were probably those mentioned previously which were so very similar to the Portuguese originals. Everything to do with them was copied slavishly: the names of the suits were not translated but adapted and *copas, espadas, ouro* and *pau* became *koppu, isu, ōru* and *hau*. The Portuguese *sota* was retained as *sōta*, the cavalier which in Portuguese is a *cavalo* (literally 'horse') became *uma* (again literally a 'horse') and the king a *kiri*. Examples of these early cards

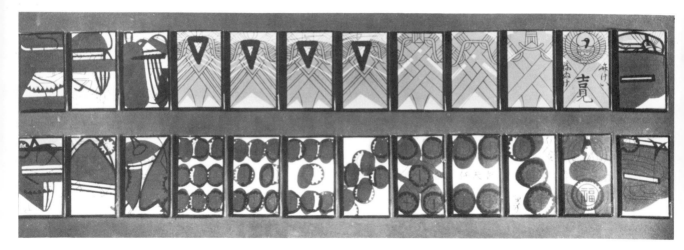

Modern *mekuri* cards from Japan (this version is called *kurofuda* or black leaves). A far cry from the sixteenth-century Portuguese designs, they still retain many features found in their ancestors. Collection Sylvia Mann

are extremely rare and most of the evidence that survives rests in the form of trays or boxes made out of old woodblocks. Certainly, however, the designs became more and more oriental as time passed. Apart from the expression on the faces of the court figures, one of the first Portuguese characteristics to disappear was the form normally taken by pips of the cup suit: the Japanese copied the name without knowing what it meant and they proceeded to copy the suit symbol upside down so that it came to resemble a money-bag with a crest rather than a receptacle for liquid. Later on the suit was in fact sometimes called 'blue crests'.

The so-called Christian Century in Japan came to an end in the mid-seventeenth century, the Portuguese being expelled and banned in 1638 although all forms of *Namban* art had been forbidden some twenty-four years before. The Tenshŏ type of playing card survived them by ten years only and were prohibited in 1648. From the time when the cards gradually infiltrated back into social custom, very little obvious Portuguese influence was apparent in the art.

The forty-eight-card pack did, however, survive and nowadays is known as *Mekuri-karuta* or 'turning-over cards' as opposed to the *yomi* or 'reading cards' such as the pair-matching game of the 100 Poets. Traditionally some of the regional patterns still made have their origins within the thirty years following the 1648 prohibitions, even surviving the later prohibitions of the 1790s. The *korofuda* type, which is used in north-eastern Honshu, is an example of this, and cards of a modern pack are illustrated above. It will be noticed how very stylized the designs have become, and very typical of a certain Japanese artistic tradition.

Such cards were mainly woodblock printed, but the full glory of the impact of Japanese art-work upon cards of Portuguese origin lies with the hand-painted cards of the late seventeenth and eighteenth cen-

186

turies. These usually belonged to a type of card known as *Unsun-karuta* in which not only the feature of six court cards was introduced but also an extra suit called *tomoe* or *kuru*, the mark of which was a circle surrounding the three *tomoe* symbols for heaven, earth and man. A complete pack, therefore, comprised seventy-five cards. (A further refinement of the original cards was the *Sunkun* pack with six suits, the sixth being an arrow or *ya*, with yet another court card and an extra, dragon card.) *Unsun-karuta* were known also block-printed, but it is the hand-painted versions which provided typical and wonderful examples of the eighteenth-century Japanese miniaturist's art. Each card was painted separately, and each card, particularly the court cards, might be designated a little masterpiece.

Theoretically *Unsun* cards disappeared with the prohibitions of the 1790s, but even today there is an Unsun club in Japan and I understand that this type of card has in fact been made at quite a recent date. It would be wonderful if, with the *mekuri* cards they could continue to represent such an historic tradition.

Dragon of batons from an
Unsun pack.
Collection Sylvia Mann

Bibliography

Javaanse Kaartspelen. Tjoe-Siem. Batavia 1941.
Ostasiatische Spielkarten. Gernot Prunner. Deutsches Spielkarten Museum, Bielefeld 1969.
Unsun Karuta. Yamaguchi Kichirōbei. Osaka 1961.
Nippon no Bijutsu (Japanese Art) Vol. 19, NAMBAN. Tokyo 1966.

Appendix 2   Hyakunsinshu and cucu

There are at least two groups of playing cards which stand alone isolated from their fellows, neither fitting into any other category nor exhibiting any relationship with other packs. They appear to have been self-generated. The more important group is Japanese, and in it the packs are devised for games based on learning and memory rather than for games dependent on skill in the handling of the cards themselves. *Hyakunsinshu*, The Game of 100 Poems, said to date back to the thirteenth century, is typical and has been well described by Yuki Yoshida, wife of the Japanese Ambassador in London in the late 1930s. In her book *Whispering Leaves in Grosvenor Square*, Her Excellency writes:

> We decided to play our national card game, which is a universal game with all classes in Japan and is called Hyakunsinshu, which means 'A poem each from a hundred people'. There are a hundred cards, each bearing the lower part of a different poem by well known poets and poetesses of olden times. The players are divided into two parties and sit in a row facing each other. Fifty cards are given to each side and they place the allotted cards open in front of them. There is another packet of a hundred cards with a full poem written on each, and these are given to a reader who begins to read each poem on the card aloud, one after the other. The players look for the card with the right lower part of the poem, from the cards which are placed in front of them and their opponents and the skill lies in recognizing from the first words how the poem ends. If you take a card from your opponent's side before they do, you can give them one of your own cards so as to decrease the number of your own, and vice versa. Whichever side has taken all the cards first wins the battle. Before all the western sports came in, this game of cards used to be more popular, for it could be played so intensely and vehemently that it could almost replace a game of sport.

'A kind of begger-my-neighbour *in excelsis*' is the comment of Sir Francis Lindley in the introduction.

The second group, which is European, is composed of several variations of an old Italian game called *cucu*, which is, or was, also played in Switzerland, parts of Germany, Austria and Scandinavia. The number of cards in a pack varies from thirty-eight to forty-four and these are always in pairs. Some scholars feel there is a connection

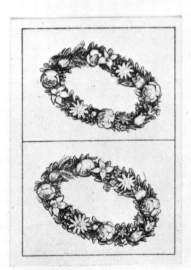

between *cucu* and the old tarot packs—Bernstrom's account of the game gives Matadors, Courts and a Matt (Fool, Harlequin, Joker).

O'Donoghue writes that a *cucu* pack consists of a double series of nineteen cards of which fifteen are numbered with large Roman figures, the other four being named Nulla, Macherono, Secchia and Matto. No. XV is the *cucu*—the bird with a human head.

The packs linked with *cucu* are: *vogelspiel* or bird's play in Germany (sometimes called *hexenspiel*, the witch game), *cambio* or *kille* in Sweden and *gnaio* in Denmark.

Swedish *killekort*, a version of the old Italian *cucu*. British Museum, London

189

Index